DAILY WORDS TO INSPIRE YOU

TOM DENNARD

ABOUT THE AUTHOR

Tom was born in Pineview, a small farming community in the heart of Georgia, like five generations of his ancestors – all farmers. He attended Davidson College in North Carolina and graduated from law school at the University of Georgia, where he met his wife, Marie. They live on St. Simons Island, Georgia, and he practices law on the mainland town of Brunswick, specializing in Wills, Trusts, and Estates.

In 1975, he purchased 90 acres of forestland on Highway 82 west of Brunswick and started a youth hostel. The property has been left in its natural state, except for the geodesic domes and tree houses, where the guests sleep. Thousands of people from around the world visit the hostel every year and contribute their talents to making it an incredible place. It is now a teaching facility where guests are taught how to live in a more environmentally sustainable way. The corporation has received a 501 (c) (3) charitable designation from the Internal Revenue Service. Please pull up the website and see the good works being done there: *www.foresthostel.com*

Tom's other published books are:

Discovering Life's Trails, a non-fiction book about many of his travels and experiences

Buzzards Roost, a novel based on his mother's struggles with Alzheimer's disease

Born a Ramblin' Man, another non-fiction book about many of his travels and experiences

Letters to Henry, a non-fiction book about his growing up in the small town of Pineview, told through letters to his dog in heaven

Tom writes a daily blog of inspirational messages to be found at: *tomdennard.typepad.com*

PREFACE

In my many years on this earth, I've learned a lot about life and how to live it. However, I don't always put my knowledge into use. I sometimes do what I shouldn't and often fail to do what I should. But the one constant in my life has been the quest to learn and grow.

Usually I meditate, not every day, but most days. For a long time I have, as well, used daily readings to inspire me in my journey along life's pathway. In my travels to various countries, I usually carried in my backpack *Be Here Now* by Ram Dass and *The Quiet Mind* by White Eagle. Reading from these books was my inspiration to keep my mind focused along whatever trail I may be hiking in my struggle to reach the top of some mountain.

With the advent of computers and email, I began sending out selections from various readings to members of my family and have continued that practice up to the present time. These daily readings were chosen as words of wisdom from sages to help teach us how to maneuver through life's tasks with less difficulty. I'd like to share some of these "daily words" with you as a teaching tool, in the hope that you'll find something helpful to guide you on your path, as well.

My older cousin, steeped in the tradition of her church, asked me if these writings are Christian. My response was, "Please don't label them. I honestly don't know what kind of label you would put on them. I just know that they've been helpful words of wisdom to me, without categorizing them." There are teachings in this book from Jesus, Buddha, Mohammed, Ghandi, Deepak Chopra, Edgar Cayce, Eckhart Tolle, White Eagle, and many, many others.

I have given credit by indicating a name at the bottom of some of the messages. This does not mean that it is a direct quote from that author. I paraphrased and merely used excerpts from the author for the purpose of illustrating my interpretation of what I felt the author was saying. If no name is mentioned at the bottom of the message, then it means that I wrote it based on many different inspirational books that I've read over the years without a relationship to a particular author or book. At the end of the book is a bibliography of authors and their books that I used for the purpose of illustrating their ideas or philosophies. If there are direct quotes from any of the authors, I placed their quote in quotation marks.

You must understand that this is not a book to be read straight through. I encourage you to read only one page each day. You need time to let it soak in before you move on to the next one. In reading the words in this book, I ask you to let your only criteria be what matters most; and that is "Do these words ring true enough for me that I can put them into a practice that will enrich my spiritual life?" I truly hope so.

January 1ˢᵗ

New Years Day is a time for reflecting over the past year and looking forward to a new one. It's customary to make resolutions about the things you plan to do better in the coming year. But too often people don't follow through. One good New Year's Resolution would be to encourage your mind to send good thoughts and good energy to your body. Believe in your body's ability to be healthy. Think good health instead of lack of health. Don't criticize your body, but think positive thoughts about what your body can do. By doing this, you're encouraging your body to be healthy, and you will naturally do things that will make it healthier. Keep in mind that the *body is the temple that houses your soul*. There is an integral connection between the two.

January 2nd

Today, as you go about your tasks and interact with others, remember that we're all here to learn lessons. When something happens that we might refer to as bad, a spiritual person would say, "Thank you, God, for giving me an opportunity to learn a lesson." Any person can do well when the seas are calm, but there's little to be learned from that. It's when the seas are rough that a captain learns best how to improve his or her skills.

Too often we treat people depending on how important or unimportant they are to us. Remember that our feelings about others directly reflect the feelings we have about ourselves. In fact, the things we dislike most about others are usually the things we dislike most about ourselves. Don't forget the adage "You teach best what you most need to learn."

January 3rd

Where is God? Too often we think of God as being up there in the sky, in heaven, somewhere away from us. But God is everywhere, even inside all of us. "The kingdom of heaven is within." Life is more beautiful when we know that God is every place that we are. We should live in reverence with everything around us, knowing that if we abuse or destroy anything in nature, we are destroying God's creation. We should live our lives respecting other people and all the nature around us, knowing that God is a part of it all.

Paraphrased from writings of George Goodstriker, Blackfoot Elder

January 4ᵗʰ

Most children want to know why they were born. When they grow older, they may ask questions like: "What is life all about?" "Surely there's more to life than what I'm experiencing." "Is what I see in my parents all I have to look forward to?" "Does God really exist?" Certainly the world has not been able to provide definitive answers to these questions, and some people want scientific proof before they're able to believe. But there comes a time in most people's lives when the need for something spiritual overcomes the need for proof of its existence. For example, we know that love exists because you feel it, but you can't prove it. Likewise a spiritual life has to be accepted on faith and whether or not its principles ring true to you. You must search in order to find it, and when you do, you should live by your beliefs to the fullest. It will make your life so much richer and more worthwhile.

January 5th

Some people need a teacher, instructor or guide, but you can begin your spiritual journey on your own. The real teacher is inside you. The entire world is your book of learning. There is a lesson in everything that happens to you if you pay attention. When you learn from yourself about yourself, out of that learning comes wisdom. The purpose of a formal education is not to produce mere scholars, technicians and job hunters, but integrated men and women who are free of fear. For only between such human beings can there ever be enduring peace.

Paraphrased from writings of J. Krishnamurti

January 6th

Don't ever underestimate that you've received the most awesome gift of all times, and that is the gift of life. Never take it for granted. This reward was given to you by the Creator to see what you could make of it. How're you doing? Remember, you have a consciousness that brings awareness into your being and gives you the ability to make choices. Try to make good choices that will be beneficial to you and to others. Gratitude for the gift of life is the primary wellspring of all religions, yet we often take this gift for granted and forget to give thanks. We should begin each day with a prayer of thanksgiving for the beautiful world we've been given and for the senses to perceive it. Don't squander this precious gift. Live this life with an attitude of thankfulness toward God and to all people and be appreciative for what you've been given.

Paraphrased from writings of Joanna Macy

January 7th

Most people, while looking back over their lives, say, "Everything happened for the best." If it's true that everything does happen for the best, then why do you have doubts about your condition or situation or any doubts about the future? You may say, "How could it be for the best if I die or some family member or friend dies?" If you truly believe the word of God, then death is not a bad thing. It's inevitable and will happen to all of us. It's not something to be feared, but to be prepared for. You must have confidence in a Divine wisdom that is guiding your life along your path. If everything had gone in accordance with your plans and desires, you would have created great confusion and chaos for yourself. Be thankful that things didn't go in accordance with your will. Surrender and let go to the Will of the Creator.

Paraphrased from writings of White Eagle

January 8th

We live in a very busy world that seems to have us working hard, playing hard, and living in the fast lane. Because of this lifestyle, we sometimes forget that we have a need to reconnect with the spiritual side of ourselves. We need to understand that we can't be completely satisfied by the success of a busy lifestyle. It's absolutely necessary to seek the spiritual world in order to be complete and whole. After all, we're not robots. We are spiritual beings. Our inner being has an acute knowledge that transcends all cultures and times. It becomes the job of the soul to seek out what it needs to feed itself. Then when our souls are fed, we will become whole.

Paraphrased from writings of Andrea Axtell, Nez Percé Elder

January 9th

Everyone must go through difficult times. It's a part of life. When you get confused and don't know which way to turn, go into a quiet place and seek the presence of the Creator within you and ask for guidance. Surrender your mind, your heart, your soul, and your entire being to that of the Creator. Cast your burdens upon the ever-present Spirit, let go, give it all up, and lay down your problems. When you insist that you, alone, can solve all your problems, it's like trying to unravel a knot. The more you pull at it, the tighter and tighter it becomes. Rid yourself of your ego and concentrate with all your heart upon the gentle, loving Spirit. Once you have surrendered yourself, you will notice that all knots will be loosened, and answers will come to help you solve the problems before you.

Paraphrased from writings of White Eagle

January 10ᵗʰ

A lot of people say they want to improve the spiritual side of themselves. But when it gets right down to it, they really don't want to make too many changes in the way they live their lives. To begin the spiritual journey, you must begin by humbling yourself and denying the ego that has been leading you around by the nose. Look at your ego from a truly objective standpoint and realize that it gets in the way of God entering your life. It becomes a duel between God and your ego to see who is going to control your life. You can't have both. Your ego doesn't really want to evolve unless it can co-exist as the king or queen of your life. To surrender your ego and allow God to take over your life is not easy, but it's the only way you'll ever progress on a spiritual path.

Paraphrased from writings of Andrew Cohen

January 11th

It's so easy to look back over what has happened in your life and say, "How could I have ever doubted? Everything worked out for the best." But the time is NOW. You are in the PRESENT while the working out is still in progress. Since you know from past experiences that things have always worked out for the best, how can you have any doubts about your present situation or your future? You're where you are by the grace of God. You shouldn't have any anxiety or worry. All that is required of you is to do the very best you can with everything you undertake and then to leave the working out to God. Some things will work out the way you want. Some won't. But if everything worked according to your plan, it would probably create great confusion and suffering in your life. Learn to surrender and have faith that everything is working out as planned.

January 12ᵗʰ

Don't judge other people or situations that happen by what you see on the surface. Try to develop an inner vision and an insight into the spiritual cause and effect of things. If you can develop a spiritual attitude, then you will know that you should never pass judgment on someone else. Practice living each day as a being of love. Love is not just sentimentality, but it's seeing good and recognizing that Divine Law is at work in all endeavors throughout your life. Try to exercise patience in the happenings of your daily routine. Patience is a sign that you're aware that Divine Law is working. Be thoughtful and kind. Experience how it feels to be kind to a stranger without any hope of anything in return. Then, practice denying your ego's power to take hold of your life. Learn to be humble. All these things are true qualities of love.

Paraphrased from the writings of White Eagle

January 13ᵗʰ

Most people want something higher than themselves that they can believe in. They often grasp
at something that gives them a feeling of temporary satisfaction. The next day this experience may
have faded into memory and nothing has changed.
They keep moving on and craving more, as if dis-
possessed. They are alone with a racing mind and
an aching heart and seek emotional relief within
the shallow confines of the self. They need more of
a reason to live than the desire for self-satisfaction.
There is a higher power out there for them that
can be reached through prayer, meditation, reading helpful material, and listening to people they
respect. "Seek and ye shall find." What is right for
one may not be right for another. But keep searching and when you hear something that rings true
for you, adopt it as your own belief and live by it.

Paraphrased from the writings of Andrew Cohen

January 14th

People are like a garden filled with every different kind of flowers in existence. You may be a rose. Your friend may be a gardenia. Another may be a daffodil, and so on. Everyone is different yet beautiful in the eyes of God. How fruitless for the rose to say, "I'm prettier and smell sweeter than anyone else, so I refuse to associate with other flowers!" You should realize that each one is beautiful in its own way? I once gave my wife a vase of red rose buds I bought at the grocery store. Each morning we'd look at the vase of roses, but the buds never opened. After several days, their necks drooped over, and they began to die. Have you seen people like that? A life that never blooms is a tragedy. Don't let that happen to you.

January 15th

When you give to others the love that you feel in your heart, this love you give will go forth and penetrate them as if it were a light. This causes a radiance to flow from your heart and from your head. This light touches the heart, the understanding, and even the physical life of the other persons with whom you come in contact. When you give out love, you also surround yourself with light that others can feel. As you give you receive. This Light force will create a protective shield around you that allows you to weather the storms of life.

Paraphrased from the writings of White Eagle

January 16ᵗʰ

You may possibly have a deep-seated urge to escape from time, because you feel it's carrying you to a final destination you dread. If you only knew the true nature of death, you'd cease to be afraid of it. And if you ceased to be afraid of it, no one could rob you of your time anymore. The more you suspect that you're headed nowhere, the faster you may run. Awakening occurs when you realize that you are, in fact, a part of the world. Since you are a part of the world and are a part of what the world is doing right now, then you don't need to secure yourself. Your feeling of lack is a lack only as long as you attempt to fill it up. But remember your feeling of lack can be transformed into a source of creative energy by becoming a part of the whole and not separating yourself from the whole as an individual.

Paraphrased from the writings of David Loy and Linda Goodhew

January 17th

They say that birds of a feather flock together. That may be true. But as human beings, there's such a beauty in diversity. There's so much to learn from people who are not just like you. You'll see beauty you never knew existed. In my travels to other countries, I've learned that basically we're all just alike. We may have a different skin color, a different language, different customs or religion, and even food. But when it gets down to the bedrock of things, we're all alike. We have the same basic wants, needs, and desires. You find love of family, need for friends, desire for happiness and laughter, sadness from loss of loved ones, and on and on and on. It's very arrogant on our part to think that God only blesses us and our kind. We should embrace those who are different from us as if they were our long-lost brothers and sisters.

January 18th

The people you know who seem to never get angry and don't judge or criticize others are highly evolved. They know that Divine Order is at work, and they accept what happens to them without a fuss or a bother. It's very human to get angry and to judge in haste the actions of others. The divine way is to remain quiet and loving and peaceful. It's true that we're all just human beings while we're here on this earth. But you must remember that you have a divine nature within you that is perfect. In your daily routine and chores, try to evoke more of your divine nature and move beyond your human side. You will be greatly rewarded with peace of mind for the balance of your lifetime if you do.

Paraphrased from the writings of White Eagle

January 19th

The security of having all the necessities of life and three good meals a day will not bring you happiness. Happiness and delight come about from the unnecessary things and the impractical. You must make time and give emphasis to those simple pleasures of life that may be small things, like eating a good meal, playing a game, creating something, visiting friends, and watching children at play. If you make your life too secure and restrained by emphasizing only the necessities and denying yourself of those things that might be considered frivolous, then you will become stale. Not on bread alone should you live but on all those heart-hungry things that make you happy.

Paraphrased from the writings of Ed Hays

January 20ᵗʰ

If you believe in a Higher Power, no matter what name you wish to call this Higher Power, your life will take on new meaning. If you're then willing to surrender your ego to this Higher Power and begin living your life in a more unselfish manner, you will have arrived on your pathway to a more spiritual life. You may ask, "How can you prove that?" C. S. Lewis said, "If you believe in God and live your life with faith, and upon your death find that it was all a hoax, how has your life been harmed? You would've lived a life that was much happier and more secure by having this belief. But if you choose not to believe in God with childlike faith and upon your death find that God does, in fact, exist, then you've lost it all."

January 21ˢᵗ

You pray earnestly for what you want. "Dear God, give me this, give me that, please remove all my problems." However, it's only by going through the discipline of unpleasant things that your eyes are opened to a greater spiritual awareness. Be thankful for your trials and heartaches, which are disciplining your soul until it becomes able to comprehend and absorb the beauty of this life. This doesn't mean that you should let go of your responsibilities or that you should not make an effort to change things in your life. What it means is that you should make every effort to do your very best in everything you undertake. Then once you've done your best, take your hands off and leave the results to the will of God.

Paraphrased from the writings of White Eagle

January 22nd

God has stored so much love inside all of us. For some, this love is crying to get out. Having love inside you can serve no useful purpose until it's given out and spread around to others with whom you come in contact. If you don't give love out to others, it's as if there is a pipe that gets clogged within you. You need to unstop the pipe and allow it to flow. The paradox is that the more you give love to others, the more it is replaced. You become like a conduit where a bountiful supply of love is being fed to you by the Creator, and you are giving out as much as you receive in order to keep it flowing. Don't worry, you can never run out of love. What you give out will always be replaced. Don't let your pipes get clogged. Pass it out to others in the same measure that you've been given.

January 23rd

You should not only show your love and respect for other people, but you should also appreciate where you are in your life. You should bear no resentment for what you have or what you don't have. It's not by accident or circumstance that you're where you are in your life. Nothing happens out of order or by chance, and Divine Order brings conditions into your life which you need for growth. So accept with love the things that happen to you. Look to the Heavenly Father each day and say, "Thank you for what you've given me." And then search for the lessons you need to learn from the experiences you're given, always remembering to fill your hearts with divine love and light.

Paraphrased from the writings of White Eagle

January 24th

"While I am alive, I want to live life the very best I can. I know I have to die sometime, but before that happens, I want to do what is right. I want to do what I can to help others. I want to be responsible for what I say and do. I am held responsible for how I choose to live my life. My life is what I make of it. God is looking down upon me. We are all His children. God is listening to me. The sun, the moon, the darkness, the light, and the winds are all listening to what I am saying."

Geronimo, Apache Warrior

January 25th

Impatience is a sign that you lack confidence in Divine Order. If you truly believe that everything happens at the right time, then you should easily surrender and let go and let things happen according to the overall plan. That doesn't mean that you shouldn't give 100 percent effort toward making things happen in the manner that you believe to be the best, but the progress of your work and the results of your work should be left to Divine Order. God has a plan for everyone, and there's no point in feeling that life should be lived by moving from one thing to another as fast as possible. What's your hurry? Slow down, take your time, and walk slowly and deliberately along the pathway that you've been assigned. This way you will learn your lessons that have been placed before you with care and consideration.

January 26th

As you grow spiritually, you will feel a gentle love rising inside you. You will begin to look upon the world with understanding and compassion. You will respect the soul within all people and become more tolerant of the spirit within them. You will have a greater appreciation for nature and animals and all living things, knowing that balance is important to sustain the world. If you continue on your spiritual path, all these things will come about. This is the generation of light, and this true light is that of love.

Paraphrased from the writings of White Eagle

January 27ᵗʰ

It's crucial to think before you speak. Make sure what you're about to say will not be harmful either to the other person or you. If you feel you need to say something judgmental, stop and keep it to yourself. You don't know the path the other person is treading. But one thing is for sure: it's not the same path you're taking. Sometimes you may get angry at another person. Rather than saying angry words to the person, learn to process your anger. However, don't keep anger inside you. It will eat you like a cancer. Spend time in meditation sending love and light to that person. Know that the inner being of both of you is divine, and you have the power to bring forth that divinity anytime you choose. Think positive thoughts, be a positive person, and try to think the best in others.

"Better to stumble with the toe than with the tongue." Swahili Proverb

January 28th

It's so easy looking back over the past happenings in your life when you see how things have worked out to say, "How could I have ever doubted?" But right now you're in the present, and you must have confidence that everything is happening in the manner in which it is planned. You must have faith that Divine Wisdom is guiding your life. After your life is over, you will know that nothing could have been altered nor should have been altered. All that has happened were things that needed to happen. If everything had gone according to your plan, there would have been great confusion and much more suffering for you. So, now is the time for you to surrender yourself to Divine Wisdom, knowing that everything will work out in your best interest as it has been planned.

Paraphrased from the writings of White Eagle

January 29th

Do you feel uneasy if you get out of your comfort zone? Especially when it means being around people who are different from you? Remember that Jesus broke bread with publicans and sinners and consorted with harlots. Do you think he did that to make himself more popular? Did he do it because he thought he could convert some of them? Or was his love rich and deep enough to make contact with that element in human nature common to us all? If you wish to move along your pathway in a much more spiritual manner, then you must develop a tolerance for others and a knowledge that everyone has a divine self inside them that binds us all together as one.

January 30th

Each individual soul has been called upon to perform a particular work on this earth. So accept the task that has been laid before you. You may long to do something to help others, and this is good. But before you can help others, you must first seek the spirit within you. You will then be able to project that special light that will make your work much more beneficial to others.

Paraphrased from the writings of White Eagle

January 31ˢᵗ

What have you been doing lately?

You've been on vacation?

You've been working?

You've been playing?

You've been working out?

You've been reading books?

If your day is spent on satisfying all of your individual needs and desires, then you are, at best, standing still. You can only grow when you get outside of yourself and begin doing good works for other people. Service to others is the highest ideal to which a soul can aspire.

Paraphrased from the writings of Kathy Callahan

February 1ˢᵗ

When you look at strangers, do you have a tendency to categorize them? If their skin is dark or their eyes slanted or they're from another country, do you pigeon-hole them? Being from Georgia, I've become aware of that trait as I've traveled around to other states. Once I say where I'm from, I can see the person's brain clicking, ready to size me up as if they know the type of person I am because I am a southerner. It's probably even more so for those who are Jewish or Muslim or African-American. If you look at people as being "other," then you have made objects of those people and taken away their humanity. You have stripped from them their wish to feel at home in their bodies and minds. Don't get lost in habitual biases that distort your feelings. Don't label others. Realize they're human with feelings just as you have feelings.

February 2ⁿᵈ

In everyone's life, sometimes the going gets rough. When this happens, you must never lack courage even though there is a temptation to do so. Don't be weary and wallow in your misfortune. Never feel that you're not worthy of the joy and happiness that life has to offer. To have doubts about yourself is the same as having doubts about the Creator. You must surrender and give it all up to God. Offer no resistance. Let the Spirit come into your life. Once you do that, all crooked places will be made straight, and wrong will be changed to right.

Paraphrased from the writings of White Eagle

February 3rd

If you'd like to expand your life and move forward on the spiritual path, then it necessarily must involve getting away from spending too much time on yourself and moving outward toward helping others. Your ego is like a disease grabbing hold and absorbing you. The ego likes to use your body, your mind, and your life for its own expansion. It strengthens itself by diminishing others. In order to awaken to the true purpose of your existence, you must put a stop to the ego running your life. A number of intuitive people believe very strongly that a new consciousness is beginning to emerge on our planet. This movement will engage us in an outward cycle of spiritual growth and expansion. If you want to be a part of this movement, you must start today diminishing your ego and allowing a spiritual dimension to come into your life through your thought, speech, actions, and creations.

Paraphrased from the writings of Eckhart Tolle

February 4th

Some people believe that spirituality is a product of the mind. But spirituality is not meant to be separate from the body. A spiritual person is one who lives fully in the present moment, which includes living fully in the body. At every stage of spiritual growth, the greatest ally you have is your body. It's a misconception that the most spiritual people must renounce the body, deny its passions, and control its desires. This kind of prejudice against the body runs contrary to the way that nature fashioned us. Nature balances mind, body, and spirit as co-creators of our personal reality and allows us to come to know the reality of God. In fact, sickness and aging are caused by the mind's inability to join the body in perfection and fulfillment.

Paraphrased from the writings of Deepak Chopra

February 5th

We don't yet understand all the ways in which brain chemicals are related to emotions and thoughts. But what we do know is that our state of mind has an immediate and direct effect on the state of our body. We can change our body by dealing with how we feel. If we ignore our despair and allow it to continue, the body receives a "die" message. If we deal with our pain and seek help, then the message is "living is difficult but desirable." Our immune system will work to keep us alive if the brain continues to send positive messages to the body.

Paraphrased from the writings of Bernie S. Siegel, M.D.

February 6th

Do you treat your body just like it was a machine? When a part is broken, you either get it fixed or get a new part. Most people only respect their bodies when it doesn't work right. But now is the time to do what we've been saying we'd start doing tomorrow. Good health is not something you can buy at the store. It's an attitude. Health, especially in an unhealthy society like ours, takes time, energy, and commitment.

"How your body feels tomorrow can only be built on today." An Irish Proverb

February 7th

The spiritual you has no ego. Its relationship to life is always unconditional, absolute, passionate, and positive. You know the spiritual you because you can feel it. It's that part of you that has the feeling of being "in the groove" or "in the zone." It's a place where your perception is heightened, colors vibrate, and the light becomes alive. It's that part of you that has no feeling of separateness with other people or with nature. It's the place where you become at one with everything. You stop using emotional drama to add thrills to your life. You are in love - in love with yourself - in love with your life - in love with everything about you. It's a condition worthy of seeking and is available to all who wish to have it.

February 8ᵗʰ

Seek and you shall find. Ask and it shall be given to you. But remember you may not get the answers you were expecting. You may be constantly looking into the future for your happiness. Your mind jumps from one thing to another. If you could stay in the present, it would bring you toward your highest good and give you peace and happiness. Offer no resistance to the present moment. Have a goal. Make choices that align you with that goal, and stay focused on that goal. Yet be grateful and accept whatever comes in whatever form. It's not necessary to make a judgment of right or wrong about the things that are happening in your life. The more you judge, the more you will have unbalanced energy in your life's experiences. Live your life in calm and have a peaceful, loving attitude if you want to be happy.

Paraphrased from the writings of K.J. Stewart

February 9th

The advantages of being on a spiritual path are many. Your life can become whole and complete. Good health can become a natural state of your being. You will be better able to release stress caused by emotional pains from your past. You will begin to love yourself more and approve of your body. You will feed it nourishing foods and beverages. You will exercise your body to keep it healthy. Your body is a wonderful and magnificent machine that you should feel privileged to live in. You will have more energy to do good works for others. All can become well in your world.

Paraphrased from the writings of Louise L. Hay

February 10ᵗʰ

In my younger years, I followed my guide who urged me to spend more time in nature. It was there that the world grew brighter and happier like when one falls in love. After learning to read the signs and symbols of the landscape, I learned to read the signs and symbols in the landscape of my life. My meditations told me that I must move my life in the direction of serving others. That was my calling. To my amazement I learned that the more I served others, the closer I grew toward God.

Paraphrased from the writings of Edgar Cayce

February 11ᵗʰ

If you've been abused, mistreated, or made to feel unworthy in your youth, it's likely that you've surrounded yourselves with barriers and walls as a defense mechanism to keep from getting hurt. Unfortunately, this can effectively close you off from the rest of the world. As a result, life loses its meaning. In order to have a richer, fuller life, you must open up and allow yourself to become vulnerable. You must believe that you're surrounded by a Power so strong, that it's beyond your comprehension. This Spiritual Power is waiting for you to open up and become a channel for its love and light and spirit to pass through you and out to others. If you choose to do this, you must clear out all the garbage and trash in your life, drop your barriers and ego, and open up completely and without reservation to God.

February 12ᵗʰ

Meditation is the simple process of removing attention from conditions and circumstances that cloud our perceptions. It enables us to experience clear levels of awareness or states of consciousness. It gives us physical and mental rest and promotes a spiritual experience. It allows us to realize that we are a part of the omnipresent consciousness of God. In order to do it properly, you must relax into the process and avoid the idea that you are trying to accomplish something. You will find that meditation not only gives you peace of mind, but it strengthens the immune system, slows the aging process, and nurtures creative abilities.

Paraphrased from the writings of Roy Eugene Davis

February 13th

This society concentrates on training its citizens how to work and make a living. Yet so often people find that their work and the life they've chosen doesn't make them happy. So they surround themselves with more worldly goods but become disillusioned to find that material things don't bring them happiness. They get a new job, change spouses, or move to a different place. But everywhere they turn, they carry their unhappiness with them. This society needs to teach people how to be happier rather than the false illusion of how to be rich. If you're not happy, you must change your mind-set. You need to focus more on living a spiritual life and free yourself from the attachment of material things. You need to retrain yourself to find beauty in nature, pleasure from a baby's smile, or watching a sunset with someone you love. You must be more forgiving and tolerant of others and realize you can find peace and joy from mere contentment.

February 14th

Love is the reason for all things - EVERYTHING. Love is the answer, the question, and the mystery. Love is what brought you into this world. Love drives you. Love confuses you. It is love you hunger for. You exist for love. And when you die, you return to love. Without love, life would be a painful journey toward nowhere. Love is not just another emotion in the game of life - love is the game of life. Love takes many forms - attraction, passion, and desire are only a few of the creative manifestations of love. Hate, prejudice, and jealously are the destructive manifestations. Plain and simple - at all times we are either creating love or destroying it.

Paraphrased from the writings of Robert Peter Jacoby

February 15th

It's necessary to have a certain amount of money to supply your basic needs. But too often you may get the idea that the more money you make, the happier you will be. Many indigenous people have virtually no money or material possessions yet seem as happy as anyone. They appear to put their focus on having close relationships with their family and friends. They talk about how they entertain themselves with things in life that cost nothing at all or very little, like fishing or walks in nature. Their lives seem to be stress-free, a concept foreign to the American way of life. Their livelihood is derived from making things with their hands to sell to others. They take pride in their work and have a sense of accomplishment in doing the very best they can.

February 16th

The Buddha, as he died, told his friends that they were to question all teachers and their teachings and to take nothing on face value alone: "You should study yourself and cultivate discernment. Where your foot is planted is where the truth can be found. You need to look deeply and see the universe in the dust beneath your feet. Penetrate the present moment sharply. And most of all relax. Use the truths that you've learned as a mirror. Let them be your ally and not your master. And realize that the greatest questions for all of you, even then, will still remain unanswered."

Paraphrased from the writings of Thich Nhat Hanh

February 17ᵗʰ

Since the law of attraction is always responding to your thoughts, a deliberate focusing of
your thoughts is important. Look for the positive
aspects of the subjects that are important to you.
As you choose a thought, the law of attraction will
act upon it, attracting more thoughts like it, thus
making it more powerful. By staying focused on a
subject, your point of attraction on that topic will
become much more powerful. Make deliberate
choices about the thoughts you think, the things
you do, and even the people you spend time with. If
you feel negative thoughts coming into your mind,
change the direction of your thoughts before the
negativity gathers momentum. Learn to be positive, think positive, talk positive, and act positive.
This will attract only good things for you; and by
doing this, you will help other people in countless
ways.

Paraphrased from the writings of Esther and Jerry
Hicks

February 18th

If your belief in a Higher Power is realized only in your mind, then that is not enough. You need to also allow God to rule your heart. You must align your heart with God and allow your heart to be changed by God. God must be present in every act that you do, even down to the smallest of things. You will find that this characteristic can be found in the lives of all the great prophets and sages. And to deny it is to deny yourself.

Paraphrased from the writings of Mahatma Gandhi

February 19ᵗʰ

You are being psychically assaulted by the media's nonstop flood of toxic waste. You are being made paranoid by the dangerous images that radiate nonstop from TVs, movies, websites, magazines, books, radio, and newspapers. The sacred temples of your imaginations have been infected by the doom and gloom fixation that so many seemingly intelligent people embrace. Stop accepting the epidemic obsession with big, bad, nasty things and take back your imagination. Refuse to be entertained by bad news. Seek out and create stories that make you feel strong and joyous. There are so many good stories and good things that are going on in the world that don't make the news. Believe that good will prevail and by maintaining a positive attitude, it will.

Paraphrased from the writings of Rob Brezsny

February 20ᵗʰ

"I don't seem to be able to understand white people. There's something about their lives that's so different from ours. I honestly believe that deep down they know the truth, but they have a funny way of burying it beneath the things that really matter. They want everything in their lives to be convenient. They want more material things than they need or will ever use. They seem to be very insecure and afraid of even the smallest of things. Most of their time is spent on things that are superficial, artificial, and temporary. They strive toward making their lives pleasant-tasting and work on projects that appear nice to them. But what amazes me most about white people is they spend such a very small amount of time developing the spiritual parts of their lives. My people know that the spiritual side of our lives is the only one that will last forever."

Australian Aboriginal Elder

February 21st

I don't understand why some people have so much more than others and are unwilling to share it. Most would not call themselves greedy. Yet, they do so little to help others who are in need. Greed could be defined as keeping something you like but don't need when you know that someone else could use it. Greed is kind of like having something extra, just in case. Most everyone has too many things they don't use or need. It wouldn't hurt them at all to share those things with someone who could really use them. Some people hoard lots of money in order to have enough to leave to their children when they die. But too often when that happens, the children fight over it and don't appreciate it. Greed is pervasive in our society. Don't get caught up in it.

Paraphrased from the writings of Anne Wilson Schaef

February 22nd

You think you're in complete control of your life. Yet things happen to you that you can't explain. You should always keep in mind that your life is a gift from the Creator. All things that happen to you each day are necessary to teach you lessons you need to learn. Once you've accepted that bit of truth and learned the lessons given you, then all your days can be looked upon as a blessing. If you fail to learn your lessons, then some days are not going to be very good for you at all. You must keep repeating them until you learn. So, you should start each day by giving thanks, knowing that everything that happens to you is part of God's plan. Then you can live each day of your life in joy with an attitude of thanks for what you've been given.

February 23rd

When you get down and disheartened and feel that your life is not worth living, remember that your spiritual guides are by your side at all times to help you. They're there to comfort you in times of trouble. There's no detail in your entire life, neither your thoughts nor your actions, that can escape them. They never judge you. They only love you with deep compassion and understanding. Remember this and don't forget it. Pray that a love such as theirs will fill your heart, so that you can look upon others with the same gentle loving kindness as your guides regard you.

Paraphrased from the writings of White Eagle

February 24ᵗʰ

The time has come when we can no longer ignore what we are doing to our Mother Earth. It is the source of all life. Everything on the planet has a purpose and is necessary for that purpose. We should never interrupt the flow of nature for our own selfish purposes. Some humans are greedy. And when greed comes into play, nothing is sacred. We seem to be willing to allow the planet to be destroyed, not caring about those who come after us. We need to love and respect all of nature. We need to learn to live within the laws of nature and not above those laws. In nature, we have the assurance of support and protection for generations to come. When I respect all of creation, I benefit because I am a part of that creation.

Paraphrased from the writings of Audrey Shenandoah, Onondagan Tribe

February 25th

As long as you continue to create, you'll keep growing and evolving. Creative people grow because they have a reason to live. The following are traits shared by these people:

1. They are able to find and enjoy silence.
2. They connect with and enjoy nature.
3. They trust their own feelings.
4. They know how to remain centered and can function amid confusion and chaos.
5. They are childlike, enjoy fantasy, and know how to play and have a good time.
6. They place ultimate trust in their own consciousness.
7. They are not rigidly attached to any point of view, although they are passionately committed to their creativity.
8. They always remain open to new possibilities.

Paraphrased from the writings of Deepak Chopra M.D.

February 26ᵗʰ

Modern education is competitive, nationalistic, and separative. Our education trains the student to not only regard material values as of major importance, but to believe that our nation is also of major importance and superior to all other nations and peoples. That is simply not true. The level of world information is high but usually biased and influenced by national prejudices. We don't need to strive to be good citizens of our nation. What is imperative is that we be good citizens of our world. God doesn't look upon Americans as being any different than anyone else in the world. So, instead of saying, "God bless America," remember to ask God to bless all the people of the world.

Paraphrased from the writings of Albert Einstein

February 27ᵗʰ

Saint Paul said we should rejoice in our sufferings, knowing that suffering produces endurance, and endurance produces character, and character produces hope, and hope will never disappoint us. So you should try to maintain an attitude that is thankful and appreciative for both the good and the bad in your life. No one wants to hear people complain and gripe about what's happening to them. So try to change your attitude. Go about your entire day with a spirit of thankfulness, no matter what happens. You can learn to meet life everyday with as much enthusiasm as you can muster. You'll see such a positive change, and you'll be much happier. Not only will positive enthusiasm change your whole life, it will make others love to be around you. And eventually you'll learn that what you're actually doing is opening up and allowing the love and light from God to flow through you and out to others.

February 28ᵗʰ

Young souls seem to be quick in passing judgment on others. Old souls, however, are more patient. They know not to expect too much from other people. They know we're all on a different pathway and that others have to learn their lessons just as you have to learn yours. Old souls also don't get angry as young souls do. They know that Divine Law is at work in all of us. So if you're a young soul, learn not to be critical of other people. Being critical of others brings about a disintegration in your life and in your soul. Instead, practice looking at those with whom your karma has brought you into association with love and thankfulness. This will move you forward on your spiritual path.

Paraphrased from the writings of White Eagle

February 29ᵗʰ

Generally the mind is more comfortable in a land-scaped park because it has been planned with an order that is pleasing to the eye. In a forest created by nature there is no order. It appears at first glance to the mind as chaotic. But the mind cannot understand a forest through thought. You can only understand a forest when you let go of thought and let your mind become still. Only then can you begin to understand the sacredness of a forest. As soon as you sense its hidden harmony, you realize you are not separate and apart from it. You become a conscious participant in it. In this way, nature can help you become realigned with the wholeness of life.

Paraphrased from the writings of Eckhart Tolle

March 1ˢᵗ

Love is one of the most powerful tools you have at your disposal. It can make bad things good and change wrong to right. Everyone is filled with love inside, but some people either don't know how to use it or are afraid to use it. It's sad to say, but some men especially may look upon giving out love as a sign of weakness. To have the ability to love and not express it to another is a heartbreaking situation. There is nothing that feels better than expressing love to other people. The paradox is that the more you give out the more you receive. Love is the whole essence of being and the reason for existence.

March 2ⁿᵈ

Have you ever noticed how you interact differently with different people? Chances are you speak to a child differently than you speak to an adult. You speak to one of the higher-ups in a company differently than you speak to the janitor. You're playing roles with them, and they're playing roles with you. These are conditioned patterns of behavior that determine the nature of the interaction. Just remember that the more identified you are with your respective role, the more inauthentic your relationship becomes. The real you is not relating with that person at all, but who you think you are at the time is relating to whom you think they are at the time. Every role-playing interaction you have with another person is basically false. So it's not surprising that there are so many conflicts in relationships, because when you're playing these roles, it's not a true relationship.

Paraphrased from the writings of Eckhart Tolle

March 3rd

Harvard University did a test on elderly men where they all spent a week together at a mountain resort. Everything at the resort had been changed to appear as the '70's - newspapers, magazines, music played, and the like. They were required to only talk about things that happened in the '70's. They went through a battery of tests as they arrived and when they left. It was incredible how much younger they acted, how much better they felt, and how their health had improved. Most everything that is wrong with us can be corrected by creating a new mode of awareness. The reason old habits are so destructive is that new patterns aren't allowed to spring into existence. Don't become stale. Change your ways of thinking and your ways of doing things.

Paraphrased from the writings of Deepak Chopra M.D.

March 4th

If you're not living a spiritual life, you should try it. Being mindful of the spirit within you makes all things like new. When the spirit inside you grows to the point that it controls your life, then you'll notice everything changing for the better. You will begin seeing the world as being a beautiful place instead of concentrating on the horrible things that happen. You will notice how much more tolerant you are of others and less critical. You will begin to love the conditions of your life. You will become healthier instead of always having some physical problem. The world will begin to look as it does after a shower of rain when you look out and see everything has been washed clean. You will smile more and laugh deeper. Others will feel the light and love emanating from your body, inspiring them to want what you have.

Paraphrased from the writings of White Eagle

March 5th

If you are beginning your spiritual journey, you not only have a lot to learn but also a lot to unlearn. First you must come out of your cultural trance. This trance is made up of assumptions of what is true that has been taught to us by society. Learning how to quiet this conditioning process is the first step in developing a spiritual knowledge. A Chinese proverb says, "Stop thinking and talking so much and then you will begin to learn." Meditation is not easy for some people, but it is essential to quiet the mind if you want to find spiritual truths. The first things to unlearn are our habits that make us ego-centered in the way we see the world and ourselves. We must unlearn and let go of our most cherished idea: the idea of ourselves.

Paraphrased from the writings of Rick Fields

March 6th

For every habit you have, for every experience you go through, for every pattern you repeat, there's obviously a need for it. If you didn't have the need for it, you wouldn't have it. There's something within people who need to be fat, to have poor relationships, to have failures, to smoke the cigarette, drink the alcohol, or have the anger, etc. All of these things are merely symptoms. There is no point in working on the symptom without working on the root cause. When you're willing to release the need for whatever symptom you may have, then it will go away. Criticizing yourself does nothing but make the problem worse. Self-worth is the answer to most all problems. Look in the mirror and say, "There's nobody like me. I'm going to start today being who I really am." There is a great need in everyone to be themselves and to let their flower bloom.

Paraphrased from the writings of Louise L. Hay

March 7ᵗʰ

If children feel threatened when they are young, they will learn to fear and to be intolerant of others. It's just that simple-fear-based education. As grownups they will attack others and dislike other people, because they still feel that sense of threat. It's a vicious cycle that propels many to acts of violence. It's so important to teach little ones to love others, to be tolerant toward others, and to feel peaceful, to love themselves, and have self-respect.

Paraphrased from the writings of K. J. Stewart

March 8th

When meditating, if you enter the silence of meditation with a high spiritual ideal, you'll experience currents of light that awaken the creative forces of your soul. They will cleanse your thoughts, quiet your mind and body, and carry you into communion with God. The vibration of spiritual light will unlock the door between the physical and spiritual forces within you and raise your frequency of consciousness. Spiritual impulses in your soul will make you aware of your true relationship with the Creator. You do not *possess* a soul. You *are* a soul, endowed with the power of creation and the attributes of God. If you will put this spiritual ability to use on a daily basis, then you will become fully enlightened.

Paraphrased from the writings of Edgar Cayce

March 9ᵗʰ

If you're constantly reaching for what you want, pushing back from what you don't want, and ignoring the rest, then you're creating misery in your life. It's difficult to get life to always work out according to your plans. It's almost impossible to eliminate the things in your life you don't like. One way to determine where you are in life is to be more aware of how you feel about other people. Realize that your feelings toward others are directly related to the feelings you have about yourself. You may perceive other people by the way they treat you. But sometimes people you like very much can later become people you don't like very much. In truth, there is no rock-solid friend nor any absolute enemy nor any permanent stranger. If you're on the path toward spiritual enlightenment, it becomes easier to be genuinely friendly and congenial with everyone you meet, no matter how different they may seem.

March 10ᵗʰ

Sometimes it's so easy to judge other people and circumstances that are going on in your life by what you see on the surface. You must not do that. You need to develop an inner vision and insight into the spiritual cause and effect of the things that happen to you. Once you've learned this, you will realize that you should never judge another person. There are too many things going on in that person's life of which you have no knowledge. Realize that God is the judge of everyone, not you. Start living each day as a being of love. Love is not sweet sentimentality, but love is recognizing good in others and knowing that Divine Law is in effect and working throughout your life. Practice patience. Learn to be thoughtful, kind, and humble. All these things are the true qualities of love.

March 11ᵗʰ

One who uses a big bundle of firewood for cooking has no consideration for the one who has to gather it. The U.S. uses the great majority of the resources of the entire world–more per-capita than any other country. Consumption of products might be better understood if the consumer had a closer relationship with those who have to gather the resources. Tribal people and those in third-world countries don't waste anything because they live much closer to the earth and have a greater appreciation for not over-using their resources. They consider modern societies to be like the rich family living in the big house on the hill, who throws in the dump more than the poor ever have. This country needs to come to terms with the fact that its citizens are all one family and should be much more mindful of not being such a wasteful society. After all, the world's resources are limited.

March 12th

Too often people want to settle the score with others by seeking revenge. You may want that person who harmed you to feel what you felt, so this is your way of trying to get even. Trying to settle the score prevents you from being open and receptive. You're thinking only about yourself and not about others. What you need to do is to neither reject nor indulge in your own emotional energy. You must come to know your emotions completely and learn to change your emotions into wisdom. You must become at one with your emotions instead of splitting them in two. Being self-absorbed will split you in two—yourself versus others. It is vital that you maintain your interconnectedness with others and strive to become as one if you want to ever achieve peace in your life.

Paraphrased from the writings of Pema Chodren

March 13th

Everyone gets sick every so often, but the Samoan society doesn't look upon sickness as just a problem with your body. In Western society, they look at illness as some sort of biological, mechanical failure. They believe that if the failure is properly diagnosed and fixed, or a new part found, then their bodies will be as good as new. They don't seem to recognize that most illnesses involve a sickness of the spirit that needs to be addressed. Even cancer can be brought about by unhappiness and a sickness of the spirit. Western society is not healthy because they focus more on making money than they do on clean air, fresh water, and healthy food. Our Samoan society emphasizes those things and understands that our bodies are more than just machines.

Paraphrased from the writings of Patricia Kinloch, Samoan Doctor

March 14ᵗʰ

There may be times when you're down and you seem to lose any enthusiasm for wanting to continue living your life. You may seek drugs or alcohol or mindless spending or other superficial things to ease your pain. But never doubt the unlimited power you have at your disposal. Doubting your life and your own abilities is the same as doubting the power of the Creator. You must latch on to that power and allow it to raise you up from your despair. Remember your spiritual guides are right there beside you and are aware of your disappointments and hardships and fears. They know when you're being tested. They absorb your feelings. Remember these things when you're down. Don't give up. Always follow that burning light within you and all will be well.

March 15ᵗʰ

Some of you are having difficulties in your life right now. Maybe there's confusion and misunderstanding and you don't know how to handle it. Sometimes when you try to unravel the knot, it keeps getting tighter and tighter as you pull at it. Always remember that the first thing you should do is to find a peaceful place, preferably in nature if it's available to you. Cause your mind to become still, go deep inside yourself, and begin meditating. Seek the presence within of the Creator and ask for guidance. Cast your burdens upon the Ever-Present Spirit, let go, surrender, and lay down all your problems. If you concentrate with all your heart upon the gentle, loving spirit, then all knots will be loosened. Answers will begin to come to help you solve your problems.

Paraphrased from the writings of White Eagle

March 16th

You should know by now that you are in charge of every moment of your life. What matters most is how you see things that happen to you. You can look upon every event in your life with the eyes of love. Or you can look upon things that happen to you with anger and tortuous emotion. It's all up to you. You may find, however, that treating everyone and everything as if they were filled with the Spirit of God will bring great beauty into your life. God is in and is a part of all things. If you choose to believe this, it will radically change your life for the better.

Paraphrased from the writings of K.J. Stewart

March 17th

What, in your opinion, is the true measure of success? For some, it's making as much money as possible. Others want power. Some want fame. But all those are meaningless when it comes down to real happiness. Let your standard of success be the achievement of joy in your life then everything else will fall into place. Most people seem to look outside when searching for what is right and wrong in their lives. But everyone has a guidance system within that's always readily available. You have the power to bring joy and happiness into your life. Don't let it slip away by listening only to what other people are telling you. Go inside and seek the advice of the Creator if you want to find the true answers.

March 18th

You are who you are, and you should be who you are. But you should also be willing to allow others to be who they are, too. Sometimes it's hard to let others be who they are since you want them to be like you. In fact, you often feel sorry for them because they aren't like you are. But that borders on arrogance. A person who is tolerant does not feel any negative emotion toward another person. And it's the absence of negative emotion that gives you freedom. Once you become a tolerant person, you will no longer attract unwanted things. You will begin to experience true freedom and joy.

Paraphrased from the writings of Esther and Jerry Hicks

March 19ᵗʰ

Our family is having so much fun because we decided to go back to our old spiritual teachings. We don't have services or anything like that. We just all get together and enjoy ourselves. When we were children growing up, the whole family would get together. Back then, nobody ever got in a hurry to do anything. We'd just sit and visit and sing songs and eat our traditional foods. But before eating, we'd always give thanks to the Creator for water, salmon, venison, roots, and berries. We'd sing songs of thanks and then sit and visit again. We have so much to be thankful for as we live our lives. And we're learning all over again how to share it with others. This makes life so much more meaningful.

Paraphrased from the writings of Andrea Axtell, Native American

March 20th

Albert Einstein was a man admired by most as being super-human. Yet he never identified with the image people had of him. He remained humble and egoless. It's sometimes difficult for a famous person to have a genuine relationship that is not dominated by ego. In a genuine relationship, there is an outward flow of attention toward the other person without wanting anything in return. Some relationships are one-sided where one wants to get what he or she can from the other and doesn't really care about the other person. Relationships that are real are those where a person loves you no matter who you are or what you do.

Paraphrased from the writings of Eckhart Tolle

March 21st

One of the most difficult things in life to face is the unalterable fact that one day death will come. Perhaps even worse is for a close family member, friend, or loved one to die. It's so sad. You may feel betrayed by God. You prayed so hard, and your prayers weren't answered. If you believe and have faith then death is not a bad thing. Our body's non-existence is as much a fact of life as life itself. Imagine a stream of water representing God. The stream comes to a waterfall and separates into droplets. A droplet represents a life. When the drop reaches the bottom of the fall, it reunites with God. Or imagine your body being a balloon filled with water, floating in the ocean. When the balloon bursts, that represents death. The water (your spirit) inside the balloon (your body) reunites with the ocean (God.) For a believer with a strong faith there's nothing to fear about death.

March 22ⁿᵈ

Sometimes desires can get out of control. We can become like a rider who can't keep his horse in line. When a rider draws in the reins, the animal becomes subdued, allowing you to reach your destination. It's the same with us humans. Don't let your passions and desires for anything get out of control. Keep them in proper perspective. Controlled desires and passions will allow you to seek the truth and become capable of knowing God.

Paraphrased from the writings of Mahatma Gandhi

March 23rd

Remember the admonition to search and you will find. Once you find your spiritual path, be totally committed to it. Read literature from those who are enlightened. Make every effort to discern what rings true to you and what does not. Respect the rights of others to follow their own paths. Don't be influenced by others who are not on the path of enlightenment. Adhere to a meditation routine. Surrender your ego to the Higher Power. Self-realization may occur fairly quickly or it may take a long time. But because it is your destiny to become self-realized, you have no other choices in life that even compare to its importance.

Paraphrased from the writings of Roy Eugene Davis

March 24th

You may think your mind is running the show, but you're much more than your mind. You've trained your mind to think that it's in charge. But you can un-train and re-train your mind to be a tool for you to use in whatever way you wish. The way you use your mind presently is only a habit, and a habit can be changed. The thoughts you choose to think create the experiences you have. Believe strongly that it's easy to make changes in your life in order to better yourself. Then the mind will make that come true for you.

Paraphrased from the writings of Louise L. Hay

March 25th

Louise lived across from the hostel. She loved to dance more than anyone I've ever known. She'd throw parties with her boom box blaring good dance music. At some point before the party ended, she'd insist that everyone get in a circle. With a good blues tune playing, she'd push each of us into the middle of the circle one at a time to dance on our own. If you didn't give it all you had, she'd yell at you because she wanted everyone to dance like there was no tomorrow. Your time in the middle of the circle meant it was your time to perform. She said this was the way life was. Each one of us is in the middle of the circle right now. It's our time to dance. Are you standing there like a pole in the ground? You better start moving. It's your life. Give it your best shot.

March 26th

Silence is one of the most important qualities of the spiritual life. For only when you are silent can you begin to hear the voice inside that is truly your own. Your inner knowing is like a mirrored pool of water. The angry or the anxious mind is like a storm on the waters. At some point during every day of your life, you must find a place of quiet solitude to go inside and find the still, small voice within.

Paraphrased from the writings of Robert Gass

March 27ᵗʰ

If you have the desire to raise your spiritual consciousness, this desire will cause an opening to
allow your greater self to descend into your physical body. When you look at your physical body in
the mirror, you may think that what you see is the
real you. But it's only a very small portion of who
you are. It's merely the shell that houses the real
you. In order to contact your true self, you should
go into a place where it's quiet to commune with
your Creator in your heart. The light that you will
see is the real you, the divine you. By opening your
consciousness to your divine self, all of your vibrations will be quickened and your body will become
purified.

Paraphrased from the writings of White Eagle

March 28th

What are the priorities in your life? What do you do that gives you the most pleasure? If your answer is having lots of money and material things and physical beauty, you might want to rethink where you're going. Some people have insatiable desires. The more they have, the more they want. It's like the game of Monopoly. The one who has the most at the end of the game wins. It's unfortunate that society promotes this type of philosophy because all these things are based on insecurity. If you're one who has fallen for this lifestyle, try looking at other priorities such as love for your fellow beings, happiness, heartfelt joy, good health, true friends, loving family relations, an eye for beauty, a good sense of humor, the desire to help others, and the knowledge that God is the source of all good. When you reach these goals, you will have security and peace of mind.

March 29*th*

We all have things we don't like to do, but we can still do them willingly. You may not enjoy cleaning the bathroom, but you can bring acceptance to it. The peace you bring to an unpleasant situation is a subtle energy vibration that flows into what you're doing. That peace is consciousness that enters the world through your surrendered action. If you cannot take responsibility for doing an unpleasant task, then you cannot take responsibility for what matters most—your state of consciousness. And if you cannot take responsibility for your state of consciousness, then you are not taking responsibility for your life.

Paraphrased from the writings of Eckhart Tolle

March 30ᵗʰ

Have you ever thought about what type of person-ality you have? If you had to describe yourself to someone who doesn't know you, what would you say? If your close friends or family members were to tell the kind of person you really are, what would they say? Are you fun-loving, jovial, and a joy to be around? If you were another person, do you think your new self would want to be your good friend? Do you find that you're somewhat cynical and too caught up in the negative parts of your life? Are you self-absorbed? Do you take yourself too seriously? If you're someone's mate, is he or she happy to see you when you come home? For the sake of everyone you know, including yourself, try to be more light-hearted, laugh more often, enjoy life, and be a person who is a joy to be around.

March 31st

One of the biggest problems we all have is dealing with our egos and being totally absorbed with ourselves. "It's all about me, isn't it?" Until you can get beyond this ego state of mind, you'll constantly be locked, not only in your own ego, but also into other people's ego state of mind. To get beyond this, you must learn that while your existence is important, you're a very small particle in the whole realm of things. You can never be fulfilled as long as you feel separate and apart from the whole. When you start realizing that you are an integral part of the universe and not just a separate person, you will begin seeing things much clearer. You no longer see other people and other natural substances as being separate and apart from yourself. You will begin to realize that everything in the world, including you, is a part of the whole.

Paraphrased from the writings of Andrew Cohen

April 1ˢᵗ

How many people do you know who seem to always be exercising yet are constantly sick or have some physical problem? While it's important to keep your physical body in good shape, that alone is not enough. Your mind must be in good shape as well. The brain is a muscle that requires exercising just as much as the body. But, like your body, your brain needs rest. There are so many negative things bombarding your brain each day such as news from the media and gossip from friends and acquaintances. Strive to reduce the flow of negativity into your mind and try to work through the stress created in your life. Meditation is the key to calming the mind and reducing the stress. It allows you to communicate with the spirit inside you. Start today by making a concerted effort at keeping your whole being in good shape: mind, body, and spirit.

April 2ⁿᵈ

Knowing that all things happen as planned, you should be thankful for everyone with whom you come in contact even though they may be bothersome. They are there to teach you a lesson. It's your karma that has brought you into association with these people. It's your test to see how you relate to them and whether or not you handle them in the proper way. Generally, if they are disagreeable toward you, they are crying out for love. Why don't you surprise them and give it to them?

Paraphrased from the writings of White Eagle

April 3rd

The need for food, water, shelter, clothing, and medical care could easily be met for every person on the planet if it were not for the imbalance of resources created by the greed of some people's ego. The goal of most of the huge corporations is only profit without regard to nature, animals, people, or even their employees. As long as you don't recognize this, you will believe in what they say. When you are cursed with greed, no possession, place, person, or condition will ever satisfy you. You will always be looking for something else that promises greater fulfillment. It's not until you look beyond worldly materialism and seek a higher calling that your life will become meaningful. You must put "things" in their proper perspective and realize that true happiness only comes from living a spiritual life.

Paraphrased from the writings of Eckhart Tolle

April 4ᵗʰ

People who spend too much time watching news on TV, listening to news on radio, or reading it in newspapers or internet are generally having an influx of negative material flowing into their brain. When you dwell on unpleasant things, you have a tendency to enlarge them by reaching into your past for similar thoughts. As these negative thoughts pour into your mind, they can get larger and larger, gaining momentum and power. Remember that your thoughts are powerful magnets, and you have the power to focus only upon things you want to attract into your life. Those who dwell on sickness have it, those who dwell on poverty have it, those who feel lonely have it, and those who feel unhappy have it. Realize the power of your thoughts and practice thinking good thoughts about yourself and others. You have the power to make yourself healthier, more vital, more alive, and more prosperous.

Paraphrased from the writings of Esther and Jerry Hicks

April 5th

Be respectful of all living things. Take from all living things only what you need. If you're going to break the branches from a tree, talk to them. They are your friends. Tell them why you need to use them. Ask permission before you take something from a friend. When I remember that trees are my friends who give me fresh oxygen to breathe, who give me shade and protection, I know that I should always be respectful to them. I should always live gently with everything that's in the world around me.

Paraphrased from the writings of Altona Brown, Athabaskan Elder, Alaska

April 6th

Our world would be so much healthier if all the countries would advocate sustainability rather than concentrating on unlimited growth. We could be a society where people actually helped each other out in hard times—sharing resources with each other rather than fighting over them. If we could just revere and respect nature as the indigenous people used to do rather than always trying to control it and using it only as a resource for development. There are some small communities around the world that are taking steps to manifest this vision. If you can't be a part of one of these communities, then you can, at least, promote them by giving of your time or resources to encourage their growth. These committed people are returning to their roots and using this power to move toward a wholesome and sustainable future.

Paraphrased from the writings of Jane Rasbash

April 7th

Sometimes you compare yourself to others and are much too concerned about what others think about you. It's not easy arriving at a point of being secure with yourself. But when you do, you'll realize you must concentrate only on two things: pleasing God and pleasing yourself. If you can pass that test, then whatever you do or say is acceptable, no matter what others may say. Some people who are into "society" can be very critical of others because they're trying to step on the shoulders of others to elevate themselves. Don't waste your time worrying about whether or not you're acceptable to "society." Do you know of any great person who ever lived in this world who conformed to the dictates of society? It's absolutely necessary to know who you are and then strive with all your might to be that person. It's equally important to allow others to be who they are, too, without judging them.

April 8ᵗʰ

No one is different from anyone else in the eyes of God. We all have the same potential to merge with the Creator who is within us all. God speaks to everyone differently, but the ultimate choice is the same for all people, no matter what their religion may be. The opportunity is always presented in some manner to everyone. We all have the same chance to be a being of love and to align ourselves with the Creator. The same teachings resonate in all faiths. The important thing is not which faith you have, but that you have a faith in the Creator with love for all beings.

Paraphrased from the writings of K.J. Stewart

April 9th

I try to live in harmony and balance with everyone I know. At the center of my being is a deep well of love that I have allowed to flow to the surface. It fills my body, mind, and consciousness and radiates out from me in all directions. It then returns to me multiplied. The more love I give, the more I have to give because the supply is endless. Using love in everything I do makes me feel good. Because I love myself, I behave and think in a loving way to all people. I forgive and totally release the past and all past experiences, thus I am free. I live totally in the now, experiencing each moment as good and knowing that my future is bright, joyous, and secure. All is well in my world.

Paraphrased from the writings of Louise L. Hay

April 10ᵗʰ

Anytime you're having difficulty in a relationship, sit down with that person and listen without interrupting. If you interrupt, your spiritual eyes will not be able to look into the heart of the other person to see what he or she really wants. Always remember, you'd rather be happy than right. A relationship is more important than an issue. An ego clothed in righteous indignation will get you nowhere. The only position that is right is the peaceful one, and if your position does not extend peace, then it's wrong. State your fears because it's always easier to give up fears than cherished opinions. Remember that your love for each other can never hurt you. Think of several things the other person has done for you in the past that made you happy. And more than anything remember that the other person is a child of God and therefore is your brother or your sister.

Paraphrased from the writings of Hugh Prather

April 11th

We all want to consider ourselves as being non-violent people. However, we do not achieve non-violence if we merely love those who love us. We only achieve non-violence if we love those who hate us and treat us wrong. I know how difficult it is to follow this grand law of love. But are not all great and good things difficult to do? Love of the hater is one of the most difficult things of all. But by the grace of God even this most difficult task becomes easy to accomplish if we really set our minds to doing it.

Paraphrased from the writings of Mahatma Gandhi

April 12ᵗʰ

There is no way for humans to prove beyond a shadow of a doubt that God exists. For those who believe, it has to be accepted by faith and not by proof. However, there's so much evidence all around us that God does exist. The beauty of the earth and the ability that humans have to love one another are good examples. Even if God does not exist and death is the end of us, the belief in a Higher Power is still a wonderful philosophy of life. The more you surrender your life to God, the happier and more secure your life will become. You give it all up to gain it all. Just believing all this, however, is not enough. You must put it into practice for it to be effective. If you'll surrender to God and commune daily with the Spirit, then watch how your life changes for the better.

April 13th

Some people, while performing their work, are so dedicated to what they're doing that they're completely free of their egos. The reason for that is their work has become a spiritual practice. They perform their work admirably without any self-seeking praise. They are fully responding to whatever the moment requires of them. They are one with what they do and one with the people they serve. The influence of these people goes far beyond the function they perform. They are extraordinarily successful at the work they do. And any person who is at one with what he or she is doing is moving along the spiritual path in the direction of enlightenment.

Paraphrased from the writings of Eckhart Tolle

April 14th

We must honor every living thing as our teacher. Much can be learned from being in nature because we're a part of nature. We live by the same laws. We're not above nature, and we have no right to dominate, control, or destroy nature. We should learn that animals are great teachers. In order to avail ourselves of their wisdom, we have to be around them. We have to become students of the animals that we've been taught are lesser beings. When we understand that animals have something we need to learn, we have started upon the path to humility.

Paraphrased from the writings of Jamie Sams and David Carson, Native Americans

April 15th

Anytime you have a problem and you focus on a solution to the problem, you will feel positive emotions. But if you have a problem and you only focus on the problem itself, then you're feeling negative emotions. This is also true with friends who have problems. When you're trying to give them helpful advice, your words need to be uplifting and not words of pity or sympathy about their plight. Your words need to lift them up and pull them out of their negative situation. When you're searching for words to use, imagine them as being well instead of focusing on their illness or trouble. Encourage them by telling them how you've always admired their strength in dealing with negative things in their life. Focusing on their well-being forces you to connect to your inner being. This not only influences their improvement but influences your improvement as well.

Paraphrased from the writings of Esther and Jerry Hicks

April 16ᵗʰ

We all must learn to deal with stress in order to avoid sickness. We must disconnect psychologically from external pressures. Learning to relax through meditation and exercise can keep a hard-driving, type-A person from having a heart attack. The first requirement is to get people to love themselves enough to care for their bodies and minds. In clinical tests, it has been shown that a negative life crisis such as death of a spouse, divorce, or losing your job can cause serious illness. When you're sad, you have a depressed immune system. People who are happy with their lives have one-third the rates of cancer, heart disease, pneumonia, high blood pressure, and even accidental death. Sometimes you can't prevent a problem from happening, but you can certainly determine how you cope with the problem. Don't hold things inside. Remember, your attitude toward yourself is the single most important factor in healing or staying well.

Paraphrased from the writings of Bernie S. Siegel M.D.

April 17th

To live freely, enjoyably, and responsibly, you should do the following:

1. Think constructively and try to block negative thoughts that distort your mind.
2. Nourish your mind with positive thoughts and positive ideas.
3. Control your emotions by cultivating an awareness of the spirit within you.
4. Refuse to allow negative inclinations to influence your mental state.
5. Perform your work and all actions with a rational, decisive intention.
6. Disregard the negative opinions and misguided behavior of others.
7. Be receptive and thankful for the good fortune you've been given.
8. Keep in mind that you're in this world to learn, grow, and excel.
9. Create an optimistic mental attitude, and you'll become more receptive to events that will make you thrive and flourish.

10. Accept the offers of those who try to help you, realizing, however, that most of what you need for your well-being is already freely provided.

Paraphrased from the writings of Roy Eugene Davis

April 18th

Many people seem to be totally absorbed with themselves. They act as if they believe the whole world revolves around them. Why do people like that have such an inflated idea of their self-worth? Generally, it comes about from a failure to put things in proper perspective. They're making mountains out of mole hills. Each person is a very, very small part of the entire network of living things. If a human body represented the whole of creation, then a person is like a single cell on that body. When one cell on a body dies, it's not even noticed. And, likewise, when anyone dies, the world does not skip a beat. It keeps right on going. So don't take yourself too seriously. Lighten up, chill out, sit loose in the saddle, and enjoy whatever amount of time in this life you have left.

April 19ᵗʰ

Suggestions for relationships:

1. Realize that couples are together for a purpose that goes beyond personal satisfactions. They are together to be teachers to each other and to recognize the divinity in one another.
2. Respect the desire in one another to seek a greater meaning of life.
3. Accept the relationship as a central part of your spiritual path and don't expect it to be easy.
4. Look at difficulties as training because relationships are a means to understand where we are caught in old attachments and identifications.
5. Have faith in the process of growth and change in your partner as well as yourself and provide support during difficult periods.
6. Try to recognize the vision of your partner's true self and assist one another in allowing it to manifest.

Paraphrased from the writings of Harrison and Olivia Hoblitzelle

April 20th

Do you ever feel sorry for yourself?

Do you sometimes feel that no one loves you?

Do you wish that people cared more about you and didn't shun you?

Do you feel down because there are things you want out of life that you're not getting?

If you answered, "yes" to any of these questions, then the problem is that you're not giving enough. Quit thinking about yourself. It's not all about you. You may say you have nothing to give because you don't have any money. Believe me, there are many things you can give that don't cost any money. If you have possessions, then there are probably a lot of things you could get rid of and never miss them. The other thing you can give is your time. Remember the more you give, the more you receive. Instead of feeling sorry for yourself, get out and do something for other people. Doing things for others will make you happy.

April 21st

What does it take to reach spiritual perfection in this world? Be gentle, loving, and kind toward every man, woman, and child and to every circumstance in your life. Be kind and tolerant in your attitude towards all the conditions on earth. Yet you must be strong to help those who are weaker, strong to speak the right word, to take the right action, and become a tower of strength and light. Face injustice and unkindness with a serene spirit, knowing that all things work out in time for good and that justice is always eventually triumphant. Have patience to await the process of the outworking of the will of God. Then you will know what it is like to reach perfection in this life.

Paraphrased from the writings of White Eagle

April 22ⁿᵈ

All things are vibrating fields of energy in ceaseless motion. The chair you sit on and the book you read appear solid only because that's how you perceive the frequency of its vibration. Everything is energy moving at a different range of frequencies. Thoughts consist of the same energy vibrating at a higher frequency than solid matter which is why they can't be seen or touched. Negative thoughts are on the lower end of the scale and positive thoughts at the higher. When the voice in your head tells sad or angry stories about yourself, you become totally identified with whatever the voice is telling you. You can become addicted to unhappiness—pain becomes pleasure. After a few hours or days of negative thinking, your body becomes more susceptible to illness and disease. You can change this only by reversing negative thinking to positive thoughts so that the higher frequency of vibration will keep your body healthy.

Paraphrased from the writings of Eckhart Tolle

April 23rd

Negligence in paying attention to the body's basic needs, particularly the need for physical activity, can destroy your health and lead to rapid premature aging. Any part of your body that falls into disuse will begin to atrophy and wither away. One of the prime problems with an inactive body is that it leads to depression. Regular exercise can help prevent depression. Exercise sends chemical messages back and forth between the brain and various muscle groups. All parts of your body need to be exercised, not only to prevent aging but also to prevent loss of awareness of any particular part. Keep in mind that your body is a temple that houses your spirit, and all parts of your house need to be regularly maintained.

Paraphrased from the writings of Deepak Chopra M.D.

April 24ᵗʰ

If you have an unhealthy desire or an obsession about a particular thing, it will only lead to suffering. No good can come from it. Take stock of yourself and think about the desires you have. Ask yourself whether or not you can live without them. Desires in moderation are perfectly normal, but if they go unchecked, they can get the best of you. Desires can lead to more and more desires rather than the satisfaction of your particular desire. In America, many people are obsessed with their physical appearance and spend an incredible amount of time and money trying to make their bodies more attractive. Do they not know that the most beautiful people in the world are those who have inner beauty? Those are the people who fill themselves with the love and spirit of the Creator, providing them with a good self-image. Whatever your passions or desires may be, don't let them get out of hand.

Paraphrased from the writings of Judith Simmer-Brown

April 25th

When I take on new eyes, I can look into the eyes of people I dislike and see a person I love. I can see the love of our Creator in them. In the face of the oppressed, I have recognized my own face. In the hands of the oppressor, I have recognized my own hands. Their flesh is my flesh. Their blood is my blood. Their pain is my pain. Their smile is my smile. I am made of the same dust. I cry the same tears. I dream of a revolution that will set free both the oppressed and the oppressors.

Paraphrased from the writings of Henri Nouwen

April 26th

Pretend that upon your death you begged the Creator to give you another chance at life because you didn't do it right this time around. You wanted to go back to earth and have another chance at accomplishing the things you failed to do. The Creator consented. And here you are. You're in the midst of the life you asked for. What are you doing to make this one right? Shouldn't you get on with the plan to make the most you can out of your life? You need to be doing all those things you intended to do. You may not get another chance. Life is short. You don't know how much time you have left. Start now doing all the things you need to do so that at the end of this life, you can truthfully say to the Creator, "Thank you for giving me the opportunity to do it right this time."

April 27th

Learn to live each day so that you are at all times a being of love. Love is not sentimentality. Love is seeing good in life instead of bad. It means recognizing the divine law of cause and effect working throughout all life. To love is to be tolerant toward others and the happenings in your daily life. It is being patient, thoughtful, kind, and meek. Strive toward having these qualities, and then you will know what it's like to have true love in your life.

Paraphrased from the writings of White Eagle

April 28th

It's never too late to start anew. No matter what your age may be, you still have enough life ahead of you to make a difference. Don't resign from life because you fear that you've become too old. The highest rates of crime, drug abuse, alcoholism, suicide, schizophrenia, and social unrest occur among the young. Yet youth is an ideal that almost everyone responds to positively. In our society, the word "old" implies increasing disorder and frailty. But your brain does not have to become senile if you will keep it active. Your body does not have to become frail if you will exercise it regularly. The body is a network of messages constantly being transmitted and received. These messages need to be positive no matter what your age may be. Keep on keeping on and keep your light burning as long as you possibly can.

Paraphrased from the writings of Ken Dychtwald

April 29ᵗʰ

If you're searching for the truth amidst all this chaos, you must maintain a clear mind. You don't want a cunning-type mind but a mind that is open and capable of looking at things without any distortion or prejudice. Your mind needs to be as innocent as a child's, completely vulnerable. If your mind is totally filled with all kinds of knowledge about things, then you'll never be able to perceive the truth when you find it. A mind has to be capable of receiving and learning. Learning is not necessarily just the accumulation of knowledge and facts. But learning is being able to successfully move from one moment to the next as you walk along the trail of life. And, in order to do that, you must always keep an open mind.

Paraphrased from the writings of J. Krishnamurti

April 30th

The Hopis believe it is their sacred duty and responsibility to take care of the earth. They know that it's a natural extension of caring for themselves. They realize that all people are an integral part of nature, and we should all care for each other responsibly. Spiritual growth requires that we have respect for every living thing. We must realize that unborn generations have the right to a world that is intact and free from contamination, and they should be able to enjoy the plant and animal life that has always existed on our planet. In other words, the world is a giant living creature that sustains humans in the way a body sustains bacteria.

Paraphrased from the writings of James E. Lovelock

May 1ˢᵗ

You wouldn't show up at a potluck dinner with just a fork and a napkin would you? Is it possible that this is the way you're treating life? Are you receiving more than you're giving? You'd be pleasantly surprised if you'd open up and start giving a lot more of yourself to others. You may say, "I'm too shy. I don't feel comfortable opening up around other people." I encourage you to be brave, step out, and enter into life with some of its happenings. You may not realize how much you really have to offer. You've done a lot of things and have had valuable experiences you can share with others. You've made mistakes and somehow managed to work through them. Sharing your mistakes with others might be helpful both to you and to them. You'll find they've made mistakes, too. No one is perfect. That's the one thing everyone can relate to.

May 2nd

The soul growing strong, the soul in whom the flame burns brightly, will face renunciation philosophically and tranquilly. For that wise soul knows that what is lost has served its purpose, and something better now awaits the soul, either on the spiritual plane or the material plane. So you should learn to face your losses in life resolutely, knowing that out of the ashes of the past, new life will be born.

Paraphrased from the writings of White Eagle

May 3rd

Some people seem to know what their purpose is. They have a deep enjoyment and enthusiasm for what they do, along with a goal and a vision. They're like an arrow moving toward a target and enjoying the journey. Stress for them only comes when they want to arrive at their goal more than doing what they're doing. Stress usually is a sign that the ego has gotten in their way, which cuts them off from the creative power of the universe. Enthusiasm and ego cannot co-exist. Make sure your vision or goal is not an inflated image of yourself. Enthusiasm wants nothing because it lacks nothing. If you have that enthusiasm for what you're doing, you can ride the wave of creative energy. You must feel yourself as an opening through which energy flows from the Creator through you for the benefit of others.

Paraphrased from the writings of Eckhart Tolle

May 4ᵗʰ

When you fear death, you're really saying that you fear you have not lived your true life. Many people suffer silently because of this fear. Yet by seeing through the fear you can turn it into a positive force. Let your fear of death motivate you to examine your true worth. Let it help you value the moment, act on it, and live in it. Visualize yourself as being timeless and that death is but a new beginning. Then every cell of your body will awaken to a new existence. True immortality can be experienced here and now inside your body. It comes about when you allow the wonder of being to permeate everything you think and do.

Paraphrased from the writings of Deepak Chopra M.D.

May 5th

Being an observer is a space in which we become unattached in order to see the whole. We no longer play the role of a victim. It's no longer about us, and it's no longer personal. Emotions are detached from thoughts. Once we accept this we can take a look at our whole process. We can actually acknowledge the whole of existence by seeing it without attachment. This is the beginning of life without judgment. We observe our thoughts as information and not emotion. This grants us a complete clarity of mind.

Paraphrased from the writings of Kara Smith and Ornesha DePaoli

May 6th

Set your alarm a little early each day so that you will have time to do the following: Upon waking and before opening your eyes, always express gratitude for being given a life, a body that works, and good health. Then meditate for no less than thirty minutes. Exercise your body for no less than thirty minutes. Practice good nutrition in eating breakfast. When you look in the mirror, affirm aloud that you are a good person and that everything is working out for your highest good. Go to your work and give it the best you have. Show appreciation and tolerance for every person with whom you come in contact. Eat good nourishing food during your snacks and daily meals. Before going to bed, read something inspirational. Try all of this for just one day, and see how much better it makes you feel.

Paraphrased from the writings of Louise L. Hay

May 7ᵗʰ

The next time you meditate, simply sit and relax your body. Once it is settled, bring your attention to your breath. At first, just notice the rise and fall of your chest and stomach. The mind will follow the breath. If the breath is deep and peaceful, the mind will slow and become peaceful. The space or gaps between your thoughts will widen and you will experience a deeper peace and a profound silence within. Let your attention rest in the silent gap between those thoughts and in the silence of the One that connects us all together.

Paraphrased from the writings of K.J.Stewart

May 8th

You're not stable like a piece of furniture that is designed, then built, then finished. You're never finished because you're in a continuous state of change. Even though you may crave stability, you have to face changes in your life. You're only who you are at this very moment. You continue to change, even though you may not be aware of it. You're moving along each day like a school of fish swimming in a stream. There's often insecurity when you're in a transitional state. But you must maintain a positive attitude and consider the steps you take in order to allow yourself to progress. Likewise, you must be tolerant of other people and allow them to progress along their pathway. Allowing yourself and others to be who they are creates a positive emotion that will move you in a spiritual direction, bringing contentment to your ever-changing life.

Paraphrased from the writings of Esther and Jerry Hicks

May 9th

If I have more than I need while others are in great need or even starving, then I am a thief. If I have something that I don't need for my immediate use and keep it, then I thieve from somebody else. I have no right to have an abundance of material goods while others are not clothed and fed. We should give away all the things we don't need to the poor. If all the people in the world realized this obligation of service as an eternal moral law, we would regard it as a sin to amass wealth. If somehow all people shared with others, there would be no lack of food and clothing for anyone. Be generous with your money, your possessions, and your time with others who are in need.

Paraphrased from the writings of Mahatma Gandhi

May 10th

The Great Spirit wants us to be in love with all creation, not just the parts we personally find beautiful, helpful, and interesting. It is fine to embrace the trees, the birds, and the flowers, but you must also embrace the weeds. There is no such thing as loving too much. Until you have loved, you cannot become your real self. Don't be afraid of running out of love. The more you give, the more you have to give. Everything and everyone deserves our love. Tolstoy wrote, "Love is life and everything I understand is because of love. In fact, everything exists only because of love."

Paraphrased from the writings of Rob Brezsny

May 11th

All humans have pain inside. Sometimes you feel angry and frustrated. You need to find someone willing to listen to you who is capable of understanding your suffering. Inside everyone there is a certain amount of violence and a certain amount of non-violence, depending on your state of being. It never helps to draw a line and dismiss certain people because you don't like them. You have to approach even those you don't like with love in your hearts and do your best to help them. You need gentleness, kindness, compassion, joy, and love directed, not only to yourself, but also to others.

Paraphrased from the writings of Thich Nhat Hanh

May 12th

If you're searching for answers to life's questions, there are many ways to go about it. You can read inspirational books, talk to people whom you respect and are knowledgeable, you can pray, you can meditate, but you never know where your teachers will come from. Don't ever think that jewels only come from those who are wise. Some of life's most important lessons come from the most unexpected sources, from the smile of a baby, from watching a sunrise or sunset, or from weathering a storm. It may even come from the janitor sweeping the floor or the beggar pleading for money. Don't ever believe that anyone, no matter how lowly they may seem, is unworthy of teaching you a lesson. Be vigilant and listen to what is being said and what is taking place in your life. True answers may come from the most unsuspecting of places and people.

May 13th

Those in the spirit world understand the sorrows and troubles of your mortal life. They know that you must strive to surrender your will and desires to the will of the Creator. You must realize that nothing happens by chance in human life. All events in your life follow a definite spiritual law. You become overwrought with fear and anxiety because you cannot see far enough along the road. Please understand that the Creator knows your needs. There are spiritual guides on the earthly plane to bless and uplift you if you will put your faith and trust in them. All they need is your cooperation of human love.

Paraphrased from the writings of White Eagle

May 14th

When you're doing a good job building a wall, you can feel the *mana* (power) of the wall. It's a great feeling to do whatever work you're doing with a focus that lets you feel the *mana* of what you're doing. In the eyes of the Creator, there's no such thing as a small task or a large task, nor is there a significant or insignificant task. There's just the task at hand. When you focus on that task, then you and the task become one. You enhance the power given to you by the task you're doing. When you are one with the Creator, the jobs you do are all good jobs full of *mana*.

Paraphrased from the writings of Angeline Locey, Hawaiian Healer

May 15th

Selections of interviews of people who have briefly died and then come back to life:

"It was a total immersion in light, brightness, warmth, peace, security. It felt like a place I've always been, and my existence on earth was a brief interlude."

"If I took the one thousand best things that ever happened to me and multiplied it by a million, that would be close to what the feeling was like."

"I knew that everything everywhere was perfect. The plan was perfect. Everything that was happening to me and everyone else was O.K."

"I realized that I was sent to earth to share more love and to be more loving and patient toward everyone I meet."

Most of us tend to look at life as being linear from birth to death. The Zen Masters know that life is circular. There is no birth or death, for that only applies to your body. Your spirit that exists inside your body has lived forever and will continue to live forever.

Paraphrased from the writings of Ken Ring

May 16th

Everything happens at the right time. You just don't always know when that time is. Your impatience wants everything to happen according to your schedule. And sometimes it does actually happen at your appointed time. But sometimes it doesn't. And that's when you get upset. When you look back over your life, you may realize that everything that happened to you was something that needed to happen. Some things weren't very pleasant but they were things you needed to learn. They were experiences that taught you the lessons that would help you to grow. Since everything happens right on schedule, why do you still want it to be on your schedule? It's just fine to relax and let things happen on the Creator's appointed schedule. And somehow it always works out perfectly.

May 17th

There are some who believe that being humble is a sign of weakness. But that could not be further from the truth. Humility is one of the most admirable characteristics one can have. Be open like a sponge and listen. Accept the possibility that someone else might be able to teach you something you don't already know, especially about yourself. If you have nothing important to say, then keep quiet. When you don't know anything about a particular subject, it's much better to say nothing than it is to pretend that you know when you don't. It is said that pride goes before a fall. But it is certain that pride will close the door of the mind.

Paraphrased from the writings of Arthur Deikman

May 18th

The first and greatest claim upon you is the claim of your higher self. Your higher self is your true self that is a shining spirit. Above all things in your life, you must be true to that shining spirit. Don't let anything that may occur in your life draw you aside from your soul's pursuit of truth and light and eternal love.

Paraphrased from the writings of White Eagle

May 19ᵗʰ

You may say, "I'm tired of this mad world and peace is all I want." Then the stock market tanks, some-one runs into your car, something that you looked forward to was cancelled, or creditors are calling you. Suddenly there is a surge of anger and anxi-ety. You accuse others and defend or justify your-self. Obviously, you forgot that peace was all you wanted. You've allowed something else to become more important in your life. Remember it's the "small you" that seeks security and fulfillment in things that are transient and gets angry when things don't go your way. If peace is truly what you want, then you will be the spirit that lives inside you. When you react with the "spiritual you," then no person or any situation can become your enemy.

Paraphrased from the writings of Eckhart Tolle

May 20ᵗʰ

There are probably things in your life you'd like
to be different. And you may believe there's nothing you can do to make those things change for
the better. But you're wrong.   Difficult things
in your life can change for the better by changing your attitude about the way you look at them.
It's all a matter of perception. You should begin
by directing your attention to how you'd like for
those difficult things to be. If you practice this
long enough, you'll begin to see that those things
you wish could be different will change in your
favor. Sickness can become wellness. Lack of having enough of what you want can become having
all you need.   Bad relationships can be replaced
with good ones. Confusion can be replaced with
clarity. You must focus your mind in a positive way
and believe strongly how you want things to be.
Then you can become a powerful, deliberate creator of your own experiences.

Paraphrased from the writings of Esther and Jerry
Hicks

May 21ˢᵗ

Sit down and make a list of things that have happened over the past week that have disappointed you. Now analyze why you were disappointed. Chances are your disappointments came about because of your expectations. Your will and your desires were frustrated. Now analyze your expectations. Do you expect too much out of others? If things don't happen the way you want them to, do you get upset? Why don't you try a new tact? Don't expect too much from other people. Don't expect that life is going to always happen according to your plan. Realize that people are human, and be especially mindful of that attitude with members of your own family. Try to dwell on the good things that have been given to you and always do your best in everything you undertake. After that, submit to the Divine Will because only God knows what is best for you.

May 22nd

What amazes me is when black people get together, even if they're strangers, they always act like they know one another. There is a closeness, a belonging, like a family. I have always envied this intimacy that they have and have wished that white people could be more like that. In my travels around the world, I have noticed that indigenous people also express this same connectedness toward other people. It seems to be related more to a philosophy of life rather than being a part of a group. Sometimes it seems to me that the white culture is built on escape from intimacy. Derek Fowell, an Aboriginal Elder, said, "White people can never understand the beauty and closeness of being black. When you're black, you're never alone."

Paraphrased from the writings of Anne Wilson Schaef

May 23rd

Do not form your religious beliefs simply because you heard them from someone else. Do not believe in all traditions just because they have been handed down for many generations. Do not believe in something just because it's found written in your religious books. Do not believe merely on the authority of your teachers and elders. But after much observation and analysis, when you find that a certain belief rings true within you, and if this belief is for the good and benefit of one and all, then accept it and live by it to the best of your ability.

Paraphrased from sayings attributed to Buddha

May 24th

Most people feel that they are who they are and everyone else is different. When you escape the trap of being locked inside yourself and allow your mind to spread out to others, you can begin to see the deeper nature of life and stop thinking solely of yourself. Compassion means feeling the feelings of others. Compassion comes by losing yourself, knowing you have no boundaries and no separation from others. You begin to think, "How can I make others happy?" You'll find that the more you do for others, the happier you will be. You'll begin to see the whole interconnectedness of life. When you become totally interested in others, you'll find that being stuck in your own feelings about yourself will become too boring. Generosity and compassion are much more fun than being tied up in yourself. If you completely go outside of yourself and into the feelings of others, then you will become enlightened.

Paraphrased from the writings of Bob Thurman

May 25th

While most people want to be happy and healthy, the great majority of people experience hard times and debilitating illnesses at some point in their lives. Those people whom you admire and look up to have, no doubt, had their share of suffering and heartaches, too. St. Paul said that suffering builds character. It also helps you to tear down your ego, put things in proper perspective, and keep you from taking yourself too seriously. Gandhi said that suffering strengthens your reasoning ability and opens the eyes of understanding. It's not that you should go out and seek suffering; but when it comes into your life, even the hardest of hearts can melt away if suffering can be endured without anger. When you or someone you love survives a serious health problem, you can come away from this experience with a new appreciation and love for life.

May 26ᵗʰ

The spirit that lives within you is a part of God. Therefore, all knowledge lies within you. Wisdom will come to those who are calm and tranquil in spirit. If you go deep within in your meditation, you will find the center of truth. You will touch the spring of all happiness and health.

Paraphrased from the writings of White Eagle

May 27th

Most everyone would accept the fact that what you eat affects how you feel. You may know that humans are the only creatures on earth who eat when they're not hungry. Many people live to eat, rather than eat to live. A Yogi guards against over-indulgence, believing that his body is the rest house of his spirit. Some say that how you eat is just as important, if not more important, than what you eat. When you become aware of everything that goes into the preparation of a meal from the planting of the seed until it enters your mouth, then you should, at least, acknowledge the work with a moment of silence or grace.

Paraphrased from the writings of B.K.S. Iyengar

May 28th

Breathing is the essence of life and of spirituality. Breathing is the link between our bodies and the world outside us. Awareness of breathing is the basis of meditation. Breathing is considered to be our connection with the universal life energy of the cosmos. Observe your breathing in a mirror or while lying down so that you notice the rise and fall of your diaphragm. When you watch, you generally find your mind becoming calmer and your breathing slowing down. Breathing out is associated with letting go. People who meditate are taught to breathe out completely by giving a little extra push with their diaphragms. By proper breathing, the life energy of the universe is transformed into human energy.

From the book, *Chop Wood, Carry Water,* Rick Fields, Peggy Taylor, Rex Weyler, and Rick Ingrasci

May 29th

Researchers came up with an experiment by providing monkeys with sweet potatoes dropped from
an airplane in the sand on a small island off Japan.
The monkeys liked the taste but found the sand
unpleasant to eat. One day a young female monkey found she could solve the problem by washing
the potatoes in a nearby stream. She then taught
this trick to her mother and her playmates. They
taught it to their mothers, and so on. Soon all
of the monkeys on the island were washing their
potatoes in the stream before they ate them. The
actions of the young female monkey somehow created an ideological breakthrough. Thus when a
certain critical number achieves awareness, this
new awareness may be communicated from mind
to mind. So don't ever feel that you alone can't do
something that could be beneficial to everyone. It
only takes one to start the ball rolling. You could
be that one person the world is waiting for.

Paraphrased from the writings of Ken Keyes, Jr.

May 30th

A sense of humor is one of the most important qualities of the truly spiritual person. It is the result of a true sense of proportion. And it is the opposite of self-importance. Real sages have a certain childlike character. If you would start every day by standing straight up and laughing out loud from deep in your belly, it is equal to many hours of zazen (seated meditation.) Playfulness, laughter, singing, and dancing will relax you. After all, the truth is only possible in a relaxed state of being. Since everything is perfect in being, having nothing to do with acceptance or rejection, one may just as well burst out in laughter.

Paraphrased from the writings of Long Chen Pa, Tibetan Yogi

May 31st

We are all different individuals. We cannot force a member of our family or a friend to do something that we feel is in their best interest. All people have their own karma to work out, their own timing, and their own way of doing things. This does not mean that we should ignore or neglect the central place of the family in our spiritual life. The family is itself the matrix of life and the source of love. Everyone should seek their own spiritual path, even if it is different from that of your family. Families may prove difficult to get along with at times. They may let us down in unimaginable ways. And yet we share a bond of common experience, a kind of love that is unique in its strength and depth.

Paraphrased from the writings of Maureen Freedgood

June 1ˢᵗ

If you were to arrive on earth from a more advanced planet, one of the things that would amaze you is how people on earth pay good money to watch human beings kill and inflict pain on each other and call it entertainment. Violent films attract large audiences in part because they fuel the human addiction to unhappiness. People who have anger and hatred in their lives subconsciously want to feel bad. They crave personal drama and negative thinking. This type of thing acts as a mirror for them to see their own insanity. Television and newspapers thrive on selling negative news to negative people. The worse things get, the more excited the reader becomes. If you will recognize this madness for what it is, even if it is your own madness, then you will begin to rise above it and end this insanity in your life.

June 2ⁿᵈ

If it's your desire to search for the truth, then it's necessary to begin by projecting thoughts of good-will and love toward other people. Try to look for the good parts of others rather than the disagreeable parts. Make an attempt to become a being filled with love. By projecting love on others, they will sense this, and it will make a positive change in their lives, as well as your own. You will be amazed at how much good you will do by allowing your higher mind and your spiritual self to dominate your life.

Paraphrased from the writings of White Eagle

June 3rd

You may get out of the shower and look at your body in the mirror and not like what you see. What you may have forgotten is that your body is only a shell that houses the real you. The real you is a spirit that lives inside your body and will live forever. When something happens in your life that makes you feel you made a mistake or that you should have done better or that you're not smart or you're unworthy, this brings about confusion. Your inner-being is saying that you are good, smart, and eternally worthy. This conflict of opinion causes you to have negative emotions. When you feel proud of yourself or love for yourself or love for someone else, then you feel good. Your brain and your inner-being are in sync. The better you feel about yourself and your abilities and the more you give out love to others, the more those positive emotions will flow.

Paraphrased from the writings of Esther and Jerry Hicks

June 4ᵗʰ

Everyone has a different path to follow. You have to find the one that's right for you. No one can show you because it's up to you. You must search to find the one that rings true. Once you find it, your guides will help you along the way. You must lean on them when you need them. Often on a moonless night, I know there is a path there, but I can't see it. I've learned if I just stand and wait, I will soon be able to see it. If I am impatient and push on then I will lose my way. Sometimes life is like that.

Paraphrased from the writings of Charlie Knight, Ute Elder

June 5th

Even when couples set out without any spiritual goal in mind, they often find that the act of trying to make a relationship tends to bring forth spiritual values. Some couples fight and love and can still create and grow together. They find themselves on a spiritual path unintentionally. They find it's more important to love what you've got than to get what you want. Some couples who are trying to resolve their differences often come to a realization that their egos are incapable of finding peace with another. They admit they don't want to be doing what they're doing to each other. They really want to love each other but don't know how. They need to let go and let God enter their space, then an entirely new relationship will emerge. "Love does not consist in gazing at each other, but in looking outward together in the same direction." Antoine de Saint-Exupery

Paraphrased from the writings of Susan Campbell

June 6th

There are many souls who may not appear on the surface to be very spiritual. But when you take a closer look, you notice how much they are enjoying life. They seem to have the ability to respect and admire the beauties of life. They enjoy and appreciate the food that comes to them. They listen to music and are raised into an ecstasy of thanksgiving. They behold the flowers and see not merely the flower, but also the spirit of God in that flower. They may not say that God is speaking through the flower, yet their souls gaze upon the woodlands and the bright flowers and from them receive happiness. They are forever touching the invisible and intangible, although they may not call it God. Such souls may not sing hymns or fall on their knees in prayer but there is an every present worship which puts them in the presence of God.

Paraphrased from the prayers and invocations of White Eagle

June 7th

So many people have a hard time accepting compliments given to them. Usually compliments are meant to be genuine from the heart of another. So you should learn to accept them graciously. My mother taught me to always smile and say "thank you" when I received a compliment or a gift. It has been my practice to accept the compliment and then return the compliment so that the giver feels as if he or she has received a gift, too. That is the way of keeping the good, positive energy flowing between the two of you, which will usually spill out to others.

Paraphrased from the writings of Louise L. Hay

June 8ᵗʰ

I teach a meditation class where I ask the students to realize themselves two years in the future as a perfect person, visualizing the best person they can possibly be while being alive on this earth. After they fully realize that perfect person, I ask them to return to the present to determine what changes need to be made in the person they are now in order to become that perfect person. Then I ask them to start aligning all of their future decisions with what it will take to make them into that perfect person in two years. You should try this on your own and watch how the changes you make will begin to enhance your life and actually mold you into a much better person than you are now.

Paraphrased from the writings of K.J. Stewart

June 9ᵗʰ

Your ego makes you believe that what you have is who you are; therefore, the more you have, the greater you become in your own eyes. Your ego makes you compare what you have to what others have. How you're seen by others is how you see yourself. If everyone had more than you, then your possessions would no longer enhance your sense of self. You could then live with simplicity and try to regain your ego by being more spiritual than others. Surely you can see through this self-delusion. It's still ego. However, by living a truly spiritual life, without the ego trip, you'd find your attachment to things would drop away when you no longer seek to find your self-worth in them. You'd find it totally unnecessary to compare yourself to others, which is the beginning of the transformation of consciousness.

Paraphrased from the writings of Eckhart Tolle

June 10ᵗʰ

What is it about our society that causes us to measure people's worth by the amount of money they make? We should learn that you're prosperous only to the degree that you're experiencing peace, good health, and love. Money does, however, give people the power to make their dreams come true. But lots of money and dreams coming true will never be satisfying to them unless they have a deeper spiritual life. True happiness comes from being content with your life, which requires an unalterable faith in a Higher Power.

Paraphrased from the writings of Catherine Ponder

June 11ᵗʰ

When you're ill or injured, don't resign yourself to the condition. Accepting it allows energy to be freed for other things in your life. See the condition as a source for growth like a salamander that loses its tail and grows another one. View your condition as a positive redirection in your life by not judging what happens to you. Develop an understanding that death is not a failure but is a further step. If staying alive is your goal, then one day you will surely fail. Learn to love yourself and develop peace of mind. Believe that you're a worthwhile person and are here to give something good to the world. Being accepting, forgiving, and learning to love is not only the best way to live, but also the best way to get over any illness or injury. Don't worry about death. Spend your time living life to the fullest. You achieve immortality through love.

Paraphrased from the writings of Bernard S. Siegel, M.D.

June 12ᵗʰ

Humans experience themselves, their thoughts, and feelings as being separate and apart from everyone else. This delusion is a kind of prison for us. It restricts us to our personal desires and to the affection of only a few persons nearest to us. Our task must be to free ourselves from this prison by widening our circle of love and compassion to embrace all living creatures and the whole of nature in its beauty.

Paraphrased from the writings of Albert Einstein

June 13th

How is your life going right now? Are you having good times or bad times? No matter which way your life is going, it will not last forever. Everything in life is transient. Nothing is permanent, and that impermanence will last for the rest of your life. Since you know this is true, then you should not take things, especially yourself, so seriously. Your mantra should be, "This too will pass." If you want true freedom for the rest of your life and enlightened living, concentrate on nonresistance, not having a judgmental attitude toward any other person or any of the happenings in your life, and experiencing no attachments to any material things. It will be easier for you when you adopt the truth that nothing in life is permanent. This will allow you to view life from a much higher vantage point, giving you the freedom to enjoy your life much better.

June 14th

Keep on keeping on. When you stumble or fall, pick yourself up and keep on going. Spiritually means to pull yourself back up to the mark. It means a constant contact with your higher self. It means putting aside the demands of the lower self. And you must continually give. Give of yourself, your talents, and all the money you can spare to help others.

Paraphrased from the writings of White Eagle

June 15ᵗʰ

Pain and suffering are a part of life. Things break, stuff falls apart, people hurt us, and living things die. We create our own suffering if we do not deal with the pain that life throws at us. We then begin to create more pain through suffering in order to not deal with the original pain. Some turn to drugs, alcohol, destructive relationships, overeating, gambling, and so on. Remember that time heals and reveals all things. Pain and suffering are actually teaching us how to love more. Turn inward, find the true spirit within you, the real you, and dwell on the spirit to find the love that will cure all ills.

Paraphrased from the writings of Robert Peter Jacoby

June 16th

If you believe that you are separate and apart from others, then you are building a solid wall around you. It's your own dualistic attitude that creates the problem. By maintaining that separateness, you will begin to imprison yourself through your own selfish ambition. To be free of this prison and the walls around you, you must give up your ambition to be an island unto yourself. You must accept things as they are. In the eyes of the Creator, you are no different from anyone else. The same God-spirit is in everyone, just the same as it is in you. It is necessary for you to accept that concept in order to be free.

Paraphrased from the writings of Chogyam Trungpa

June 17ᵗʰ

I lived with an Aboriginal tribe in Australian. Their only security was the sun coming up in the morning and setting each evening. There was nothing else in their lives that they knew for sure would happen. Yet they suffered no ulcers, no hypertension, nor any cardiovascular problems. In western society, we go to great lengths to make ourselves as secure as we can, yet we are subject to all those unhealthy conditions. Our whole concept is to try to make the universe motionless so that we feel safe instead of trying to learn to live with a universe that is evolving and ever-changing. We try to stop evolution and make life stand still for our own security. No wonder this stresses the body! Healthy people, like the Aboriginals, learn to live with their world as it is and adjust to the ever-changing conditions.

Paraphrased from the writings of Marlo Morgan

June 18th

Blessed are the meek for they shall inherit the earth. Who are the meek? They are those who no longer have egos who have awakened to their essential true nature as consciousness. They recognize that there is a consciousness in all life-forms. They live in a surrendered state and feel a oneness with the whole world and its source. Their awakened consciousness will strive to make the necessary changes on our planet. A new species is arising right now on this earth. They are the meek who understand that they are a part of all peoples and a part of all living things.

Paraphrased from the writings of Eckhart Tolle

June 19th

You are the truth. If you look for it elsewhere, you will be deceived. The truth is the essence within all of us, in fact, within every life form. Christian mystics called it the Christ within, Buddhists call it your Buddha nature, and Hindus call it the Atman, the indwelling God. Being in touch with that dimension of yourself is your natural state, not some miraculous achievement. Those who don't get in touch within themselves seem to be more into laws, commandments, rules, and regulations. "Love and do what you will," said St. Augustine. Words cannot get much closer to the truth than that.

Paraphrased from the writings of Eckhart Tolle

June 20th

People are not like pieces of furniture that are first designed, then created, then finished. People are more in a state of movement, ever changing all the time, whether or not they are aware of it. Hopefully, your movement is focused on a state of spiritual growth. Yet, at any given time, you are who you are at that particular moment. Any time you are in a state of positive emotion you're allowing yourself the opportunity to progress. It's also an aid to progress to be in a state of positive emotion toward other people. Give them the opportunity to progress as well by allowing them to be the people they really are. A positive attitude toward yourself and others will spiral you forward and upward to a much better state of being.

June 21ˢᵗ

Do you ever think of yourself as a magnet? Sometimes when you think about something a lot, you get it, whether it's good for you or not. Your thoughts are very powerful. They have a tendency to attract. Those who believe themselves to be in good health and send their body good vibrations generally have good health. On the other hand, those who worry a great deal about their health and believe themselves to be in poor health are sick a great deal of the time. Those who believe themselves to be poor attract poverty. Those who believe they're rich and filled with a multitude of blessings will have a happy and fruitful life. Your life experiences are what bring you knowledge and wisdom. So today concentrate on thinking good thoughts. Use your powers to surround your earthly body with loving vibrations, filled with an abundance of good health.

Paraphrased from the writings of Esther and Jerry Hicks

June 22nd

At times it seems that bad things are happening to you. And so often there are troubles in human relationships. Humans don't seem to learn lessons by being told what is best for them. They have to be shown sometimes with a harsh reality. Lessons are better learned by experience. The spiritual world always takes the longer view of a situation. Humans seem to look at things with their noses pressed against the window-pane. Those in the spirit world know that eventually all crooked places will be made straight and all injustices will be righted.

Paraphrased from the writings of White Eagle

June 23rd

No matter what words you may speak to young people, they learn more from what you do rather than what you say. You may speak at great length about having a person who doesn't waste or harm the environment in any way, yet when young people see what you actually do on a day-to-day basis, they may see another story. They look up to you and want to learn from you. When have you shown them the beauty of nature, the magnificence of trees and shrubs and flowers and God's creatures? It's one thing to insist on a formal education in school, but there's so much more to learn by being close to the earth. "One who meditates on life and its meaning, and accepts the kinship of all creatures, and acknowledges unity with all things in the universe, finds the true essence of civilization." Chief Standing Bear, Sioux

June 24th

A rich young man asked Jesus, "Good Teacher, what must I do to inherit eternal life?" Jesus responded, "Go, sell what you have, and give to the poor, and you will have treasure in heaven." The young man went away sorrowful because he had great possessions. Jesus then said to his disciples, "How hard it will be for those who have riches to enter the kingdom of God!" This is really the story of mankind in general. There is nothing inherently evil about having money and great possessions, but the evil comes from the attachment you have to your money and possessions. Do not think that it means only material possessions, but it also encompasses preconceived ideas, over-confidence in your own judgment, spiritual pride, habits of life that you refuse to renounce, overly-concerned about respect from others, fear of public ridicule, as well as desire for worldly honor and distinction. These are the possessions that keep you chained to the rock of suffering and exiled from the spirit of God.

Paraphrased from the writings of Emmet Fox

June 25ᵗʰ

Non-judgmental justice is a perception that allows us to see everything in life without engaging our negative emotions. It relieves us from having the self-appointed jobs of judge and jury. We realize that nothing escapes the law of karma. This brings forth understanding and compassion for things that happen to us. Gandhi was beaten but refused to prosecute his attackers because he saw they were doing what they thought was right. Jesus asked forgiveness, not vengeance, for those who tortured him and placed him on the cross. Within this framework of being non-judgmental, we evolve as individuals and as a species. We take away our power of judging which has the effect of empowering us as human beings.

Paraphrased from the writings of Gary Zukav

June 26th

You may not be aware of it, but you play a large part in creating your own experiences. Why not try it and see what happens? As each segment of your day changes, stop and say to yourself how you'd like the next segment to be. Once you make the determination, add emphasis to what you've planned. Take, for example, that you have a car and that you have to be at a certain place at a particular time. Before you begin, stop and think for a moment how you'd like for this journey to be. Do you want music playing or do you prefer quiet? Is the weather ideal enough to let your windows down and enjoy the fresh air? Let your imagination run away with you. Then do this with the next segment of your day and so on. You'll be surprised how much this will enhance your day and make your life more enjoyable.

June 27th

Love thy neighbor as thyself may well be the single most powerful bit of medical advice any of us could ever follow. Love is the physician of the universe because it has the power to heal all ills. Love is more than an emotion or spiritual quality. It is a healing power that exists for everyone. All of us have experienced the soothing and healing effect of love. Negative feelings close down the immune system, while positive feelings turn it on to its optimum. Grief from loss of a loved one and depression make us more susceptible to illness, while expressing love for others improves immune efficiency. You have so much love inside you that is not being used, so start using it. There will be an incredible amount of positive experiences that will flow from it.

Paraphrased from the writings of Catherine Ponder

June 28th

Even though we don't sometimes feel like it, we should reach out and care for our family members. As we give of ourselves to other family members, we grow in caring, tolerance, and understanding. The healthiest families make deliberate decisions to invest time and energy in their relationships. Recalling good memories of family experiences, reliving familiar traditions, and retelling family stories keep the family connected and its spirit alive. Families should always try to work out their problems with each other rather than walking away from problems. Family members should never hold grudges but should reach out to one another with love and forgiveness. Learn to say, "Will you forgive me? I really hurt you, and I'm sorry." The most wonderful gift we can give each other is to accentuate the positive. Tell your family members you love them with your words, your looks, your touch, your attitude, and with your thoughtfulness.

Paraphrased from the writings of Donald and Nancy Tubesing

June 29th

You must be true to life by being true to your inner purpose. If you will start doing everything you do with only the present in mind, your actions will become charged with spiritual power. It may not be necessary to change what you do, but just change how you do it. If you will stay in the now, consciousness will begin flowing into what you do. What you want to achieve through the act of doing your task will suddenly become secondary. Everything in the past was always done with the notion of purpose, always associated with the future or the outcome of what you were doing. By leaving your mind in the present, a deeper purpose will surface that can only be found through the denial of time.

Paraphrased from the writings of Eckhart Tolle

June 30*th*

No matter what your occupation may be, remember that whatever it is, it's your form of service. And you should treat your work as if you're a servant for those whom you serve. If done with the right attitude, your work on earth can make a contribution to the happiness of all. To accomplish this, it's necessary to allow the Creator to become a part of your work–hand in hand. Then be thankful for every opportunity you've been given to serve others.

Paraphrased from the writings of White Eagle

July 1ˢᵗ

It's so important to know who you are, but sometime this is colored by how you perceive that others treat you. You may say, "I get no respect, attention, or recognition. People take me for granted and nobody loves me." If you believe this, then it will not only discolor your self-respect, but also you will be forever lacking. This misperception will create a dysfunction in all your relationships. You can change this by starting to focus on abundance. Make a daily practice of acknowledging all the good things in your life. Always be thankful for what you have. If you think that others are not treating you right, then practice giving to them what you feel they're not giving to you. If you're not getting enough praise and appreciation from certain people, then start giving out praise and appreciation to them. As soon as you start giving, you will start receiving.

July 2nd

If you wish to serve adequately and become as good a person as you can be in this lifetime, you must make sacrifices. You must sacrifice your uncontrolled desires, and you must make sacrifices of yourself. Many of those who have become masters have even sacrificed life itself. There is no true service without sacrifice. You may shrink from it, but you cannot alter the law of life. You must first fill your heart with love, not only for yourself but for all living beings and for the whole earth. Realize that you are one with everything. Then all of your service and all of your sacrifices will bring you such joy, you will not feel that it is a sacrifice.

Paraphrased from the writings of White Eagle

July 3ʳᵈ

Being who you are is being at peace. Typically, people make the following statements: "Something needs to happen in my life before I can be at peace." "Something happened in my past that keeps me from being at peace." "Because of the situation I'm in right now, there is no way I can be at peace—maybe later." You must learn that your only opportunity for peace is to find it right now. You have to make peace with the present moment with things just as they are. You may be making yourself suffer and others around you suffer without even knowing it. You can only find that peace now if you rid yourself of the ego that drives you. Your ego needs to cease forming the basis for your identity and just be yourself without the ego.

Paraphrased from the writings of Eckhart Tolle

July 4th

The most wonderful gift we can give to one another is affirmation. Say "I love you" as often as you can. Don't just assume that others know you care for them—let them know. Don't be stingy with your love. Tell your family and your friends you love them with your words, your looks, your touch, your attitude, and your thoughtfulness. When you tell a friend or family member you love them, focus on the qualities that make that person unique. Tell them what you appreciate about them. Treat strangers with courtesy, respect, and interest as if they were your friends. These positive ways of living will not only benefit everyone around you but also will benefit you as well.

Paraphrased from the writings of Donald and Nancy Tubesing

July 5th

If we can free ourselves from being constantly imprisoned by time, then life can become more playful and enjoyable. Play is what we're doing when we don't need to gain something from a situation. When we can come to the point that we don't devalue the present in order to extract something from it, there will be time to do our work with pride and loving care. We'll begin to have friendly chats with people in whom we have a genuine interest. On our way to work, we'll have time to look at the scenery and perhaps find something beautiful in nature to admire. In our work, we'll devote our time to doing our jobs with pride and loving care and stop trying to turn out as much work as we can in the shortest possible time.

Paraphrased from the writings of David Loy and Linda Goodhew

July 6ᵗʰ

"The more one can experience the common thread connecting all things, the closer one comes to the subtle conscious essence which is all-permeating.

"Everything is contained within everything. The spirit of God exists within all people.

"We have to reap the fruits of our own actions and experience the results of the person we really are.

"If we think negative thoughts toward others, we are really hurting ourselves.

"One gives one's own thoughts power. The wise witness their thoughts and empower only those that are beneficial. Seeing the positive side of things helps to bring forth positive qualities within oneself.

"You never have any reason to feel self-righteous about anything since whatever good is done in the world is done by God through whomever He chooses."

Quotes from *God Alone Is*, Shankar Das

July 7ᵗʰ

How often each day do you sing? Too often people in the western world don't sing at all except maybe in their religious worship. Singing is not just music; it also represents rhythm and order. The effect of singing is like an electrical charge to your emotional health. It's not only soothing, it's also healing. Indigenous people sing frequently as they work. They sometimes sing alone but often sing in unison with other workers. Perhaps they sing as they labor to ease the pain. This practice has such a healing effect on them. You should make it a compulsory practice to sing at least once every day. Try it and see if it makes a difference in your attitude.

July 8th

You may think, "I'm just one person, and what can one person do to make a difference?" This may surprise you, but you have the power to help the whole world. The thing you can do is waiting there in your own heart every day. The greatest service that anyone can give to the world is to always think aright by continually sending forth the love you have in your heart to others and always be willing to forgive.

Paraphrased from the writings of White Eagle

July 9th

Emotional pain lives within most human beings. It has its own primitive intelligence like a cunning animal. The pain-body is not just individual in nature but it takes on suffering throughout the history of humanity. It periodically needs to feed in order to take in new energy. It thrives on negative thinking as well as melodrama in relationships and is addicted to unhappiness. When this pain-body takes over, people want others to be just as miserable as they are. You can only go beyond it by taking responsibility for your inner state. As long as you blame others, you keep feeding the pain-body and remain trapped in your ego. The only cure is true forgiveness. With forgiveness, you no longer feel like a victim and your true power emerges. Instead of blaming the darkness, you bring in the light.

Paraphrased from the writings of Eckhart Tolle

July 10th

Of all the teachers I've ever known, I've never found a single one greater than trees. If I'm having a rough time, trouble coping with life, or need a little inspiration, I go sit under a tree. Not just any tree, but an old, gnarled one with missing limbs and knotholes. I lay my head against a great root and fall asleep to the lullaby of the wind through the leaves. If I keep doing this over and over, I'll eventually find my answers. It worked for Buddha and countless other seekers. When life is hard, reach for the light, reach for where you're rooted. Grow through whatever hardship comes your way. Stay rooted and strive, even though you may never grasp your goals. You will attain something greater—your true self. You will fulfill yourself and add something of value and beauty to the world.

Paraphrased from the writings of Douglas Wood

July 11th

In your workplace, try to keep your business alive, always changing to keep up with new technology and the changes of the times. Practice tolerance and compassion with your co-workers and encourage personal growth in their lives. Try to create a happy workplace that comes from a challenging and satisfying relationship with your work. Be truthful but not ever critical of others. Care about and take pride in the product you produce. Don't let money be the only reason you work. If so, it's not worth doing. Remember that the end never justifies the means, for in reality it's not the end you are seeking, but the execution that is important. Keep your life outside your work alive and diverse and fun. Be playful and cheerful, and, above all, don't take yourself too seriously.

Paraphrased from the writings of Mirabai Bush

July 12th

I need to know who I am. I need to know where I came from. I need to know that I don't have to live my life in isolation. I need to know that I have the blood of my ancestors in my veins. I need to know that I have the wisdom of the elders in my brain. I need to know that I have the truth of my Creator in my soul. I don't need to own land or have lots of money, only enough to meet my needs. My needs are very simple. It doesn't take much for me to be happy. I need to have my place to go in nature where I can talk to my Creator. Without this, I am alone.

Paraphrased from the writings of Oren Lyons, Onondaga Tribal Chief

July 13ᵗʰ

I've found that if you really desire something for your highest good, you will receive it. However, most of the time it doesn't come in the way you expect it or in the form you had hoped for. You must remain open to everything that comes into your life and find the beauty in all things.

Attributed to the words of Mohammed

July 14ᵗʰ

"What about the people who've hurt me?" As hard as it may seem, there's no way to ever get over hurts until you learn to forgive. Remember, forgiveness does not mean condoning the wrong. To forgive, you must pray for that person and then pray for yourself to give you the necessary strength. In prayer and meditation, you should send forth love, light, and Holy Spirit to the wrongdoer. Visualize that you are surrounding that person with light. Pray for his or her well-being and then ask forgiveness for that person. If you will do this daily, you will lose the anger and heal the hurt. But you must also remember to pray for yourself as well and ask forgiveness for yourself. This will give you freedom from the burden of carrying those hurts around, allowing you to move forward on your spiritual path.

July 15th

Those in the outer world know that you are moving along your path that is governed by a divine law. The purpose of the law is to draw all people together into a consciousness of God. Never look backwards unless it is to acknowledge how beautiful and blessed your pathway has been. Remember that you are moving forward, travelling life's path to find happiness once again, and this time it will be a happiness beyond your imagination.

Paraphrased from the writings of White Eagle

July 16th

"It is God's master plan for each one of His creatures to do its own thing, that is, for the cell to grow and continue to multiply, the plant to flourish and reseed through the processes of nature, and man to learn and develop through his faith in God and the full use of his foreordained talents and abilities. It is not the kind of talent He has given you in His divine design but what you do with it that is important. If you are using your talent to the very best of your ability and are in spiritual harmony with your Creator and fellow human beings through faith, then you are doing great things in the eyes of God, no matter how others may evaluate your achievements."

Quote from *The Call to Glory*, Jeane Dixon

July 17ᵗʰ

Most people who are employed spend the majority of their waking hours at their workplace. While you may not be the boss, there are certain things you can practice to make your work better. One thing you can do is to practice compassion and empathy for your co-workers and your customers or clients. Care about the product you produce and encourage your co-workers to do the same. Always tell the truth, even when a lie might seem to work better. A paycheck should be your reward for doing a good job and not the focus of why you're there

July 18th

If you would only let go of your desire to control and allow the Great Spirit to take over your life, all would be whole and complete. If there's resistance inside you that prevents you from doing this, then you need to release it and let it go. You need to affirm that you're the power in your world. Go with the flow of changes that take place in your life as best you can. Look in the mirror and say, "I approve of myself and the way I am changing, and I am doing the best I can." You will then get into the rhythm and flow of your ever-changing life. Then all will be well in your world.

Paraphrased from the writings of Louise L. Hay

July 19ᵗʰ

Complete enlightenment is the permanent recognition of yourself as not being separate from anything. Enlightenment is the experience of expanding our consciousness beyond its present limits. When you identify with the peace within you, you become peace. When you identify with your ego, you have a tendency to attach your sense of self to the things in the world around you. If you do that, ego will run the show because your peace depends on all external things staying the same, and they don't. A wise sage once said that you should build your house on the rock of inner peace and not on the mud of a fearful ego.

Paraphrased from the writings of K.J.Stewart

July 20ᵗʰ

I asked God, "Why do You allow some people to have so much money and material things, yet others have nothing and are living in poverty?" God responded, "I was just about to ask you the same question."

If you were one of ten children in a family, seven had plenty, and three had nothing, what would you do if you were one of the seven? Wouldn't you be willing to share some of what you had with your brothers and sisters who had nothing? Remember that all the people on this planet are members of God's family. Share your abundance with others, and don't do this out of a feeling of guilt. Once you've given, you'll find that it brings you great joy. The best thing you can do with your material goods is to give some to those who don't have much. It truly is better to give than to receive.

July 21ˢᵗ

Try to think of yourself as being natural, loving, and simple. The more simple you are, the nearer you will be to the realization of the nature of the Spirit world. Try to focus on things that are good for others and good for society and not just yourself. Fill your heart with love and have patience with your every-day encounters.

Paraphrased from the writings of White Eagle

July 22nd

In the Native American culture everything is geared toward the children. They learn respect because they're shown respect. They're allowed to be free, yet there's always someone there close by to teach them how to act. They're taught the right way to treat other people. They're taught to be generous, to be respectful to all people, and to love all living things. They're taught to believe in the Creator and the Great Circle of Life. So they know that everything comes back to where it started.

Paraphrased from the writings of Matthew King

July 23rd

You can feel that you have an abundance of blessings in your life if you're grateful for everything you have rather than focusing on what you don't have. By practicing thankfulness in your daily activities, it will train you to see all of life as an opportunity. Even when life deals you something you don't like, you will learn that life is still a gift. Then you'll be better able to deal with negative things that happen to you. Life may not always seem pleasant, but your attitude toward life is the thing that can change all that.

Paraphrased from the writings of Rick Fields

July 24ᵗʰ

In Maori tradition, there's a word called "aroha." It's best defined as a feeling of unconditional love derived from the presence and breath of the Creator. It's a word rarely talked about or mentioned in any way. It is too sacred and divine to be spoken with human words. It's something that can only be practiced. It is best described by my elder like this: "I have known aroha and have given aroha. I know it when I feel it, but I can't make it happen. I can only be open to it and allow it to happen on its own. I must continually be aware of anything going on in my life that might prevent me from giving and receiving aroha. I wish everyone in the world could learn to be open for giving and receiving aroha. It would revolutionize the whole world."

Paraphrased from the writings of Rangimarie Turuki Pere, Maori Writer

July 25^{*th*}

The truest test of your worth is not your clothing or what you possess, but it is your character. Your character is even more important than your education, and it is the main thing you should pass along to your children. To build your character, you must attain mastery over your thoughts and actions. Character does not come from anything external, it comes from within.

Paraphrased from the writings of Mahatma Gandhi

July 26ᵗʰ

Have you ever thought what you'd do if you knew this was the last day of your life? Are there things left undone you'd like to do? Are there things left unsaid you'd like to say? Are there any wounds that need to be healed? Are there friendships that need to be rekindled? Is there anyone who needs to hear you say, "I love you?" Why not do all those things you've left undone? Why put it off? Think of this day as being your last. Have you failed to live life to the fullest? Then what are you waiting on? If you don't like something, change it. If you can't change it, then change the way you think about it.

July 27th

As many times as possible during the day, breathe in and out as slowly and as deeply as you can. Try to relax your mind and your body. As you do this, imagine that you're filling every particle of your being with the love and light of the Holy Spirit. As this love and light and spirit fills up your heart and mind, every cell of your body will be transformed.

Paraphrased from the writings of White Eagle

July 28th

You're told you should surrender it all to God. The word "surrender" brings up images of defeat and weakness in our culture. But true surrender is not like giving up the ship to the enemy. Surrender is something that is at the heart of a spiritual life, as well as any loving relationship. From a spiritual standpoint, surrender is openness and a willingness to receive. It means giving up control and your ego and turning it over to a Higher Power. It doesn't mean giving up your power. In fact, you increase your own power by surrendering. When you're willing to receive, it means you're taking in more love. And when you're taking in more love, you're taking in more independence, more freedom, and more spiritual power. Several times a day, stop, breathe deeply, and surrender your body, your mind, your heart, your strength, your ego, and your whole life to the Creator.

Paraphrased from the writings of Sondra Ray

July 29ᵗʰ

True love is not primarily a relationship to a specific person. It is much more of an attitude that is determined by your relationship to the world as a whole and not toward one object of love. In order to truly love another person, you must love all people, you must love the world, and you must love your own life. When you say to another person, "I love you," what it really means is, "I love everybody in you, I love the world through you, and I love myself in you."

Paraphrased from the writings of Erich Fromm

July 30ᵗʰ

It's necessary to have a spiritual foundation upon which to base your life so that you can withstand the tests of life that are given to you. You need a Higher Power to help you along when you're growing older, when you have a marriage crisis, a financial crisis, or a crisis that one of your children has encountered. But unfortunately we live in a society where spiritual values are eroding. This makes it even more important for parents to develop a spiritual foundation on which to base their lives. In this society, people work hard to accumulate material things to pass on to their children when they die, thinking that this is the best thing they can do for them. But, by far, the most valuable assets you can pass on to your children are good values, a good philosophy of life, and a solid spiritual foundation.

Paraphrased from the writings of Dr. Ross Campbell

July 31ˢᵗ

If you're frustrated because you haven't found the right pathway for your life, be patient. You can look at others and see what they're doing, but in the final analysis, you must establish your own path. Before setting out, you must be aware that the thing you call your body is not the real you. In fact, it's only a very small part of who you really are. The real you is a spirit that lives inside your body in the same way a snail lives inside a shell. Your body may be weak, sick, or injured, and will eventually die. But your spirit will never die. It will live forever as one with the Creator. The kingdom of heaven is within. You need to go inside yourself and call upon the Spirit. Once you've made the connection, you'll always have a companion to accompany you on your journey through life, one who'll help you find your way.

August 1ˢᵗ

Life is a very special gift that should never be taken for granted. As often as possible you should give thanks to the Creator. In a spare moment during your day, just say, "Thank you, God, for giving me a life, and help me to live it to the fullest according to Your will." By doing this, it will make you more appreciative of all the good things you have in your life. Try your best to be thankful even when the day is not going so well. The problems of life are necessary ingredients to make you strong. So be thankful that you are being strengthened when times are hard. Living a life of thankfulness will grow to become a habit. It will not only improve your attitude and disposition, but it will make you have a much happier life.

August 2nd

Most everyone says that what they really want in life is to be happy. It has been said that happiness is a sign of intelligence. If you're really smart then you should be smart enough to make yourself happy. But true happiness is the result of being thankful for what you've been given, without constantly searching for something new and different outside. Keep in mind that you can never find true happiness without a strong faith in the Divine Power. You must realize that you must do your very best in everything you undertake, always keeping in mind that some Higher Power much greater than you is guiding you along the way. This will bring to your soul perfect and indescribable happiness.

Paraphrased from the writings of White Eagle

August 3rd

The true destiny in life is for all people on the planet to become awakened to their spiritual purpose. This sounds like an impossible pipe dream, but it's achievable if everyone would focus their lives in that direction. You may say that something like that could never happen, yet anything is possible through the grace of God. You can achieve certain things in life through struggle, determination, and sheer hard work. But there is little joy in that, for ultimately it all ends in some form of suffering. If you want to truly live and start the awakening process in your life, first get rid of your ego. It's the stumbling block in your life that is standing in the way. Next, you must surrender completely to the Higher Power. By doing these things, your life and you will begin to fulfill your true destiny.

Paraphrased from the writings of Eckhart Tolle

August 4th

The greatest force in the human body is the natural drive of the body to survive. But that force is not separate and apart from the belief system, i.e., the mind. The mind can actually translate expectations into physiological change. The fifteen billion neurons in the human brain have the ability to convert thoughts, hopes, ideas, and attitudes into chemical substances. Everything begins with belief. What you believe is the most powerful weapon you have. You should use it in ways that not only benefit your mind, body, and spirit, but others as well.

Paraphrased from the writings of Norman Cousins

August 5th

Most of us like to play games and especially enjoy it if we can win. But how good are we at playing the game of life? Are we playing to win? The playing field is the earth, and the game lasts for the length of our life. The point of the game is to achieve enlightenment, awareness, love, or realization, or whatever we conceive as our highest and ultimate goal. It is the largest and most serious game on the planet. It is so real that we tend to forget, in the heat and excitement of play, that we're actually playing this game. But if we play with the right spirit, it will be the most enjoyable and satisfying game of all.

Paraphrased from the writings of Rick Fields

August 6ᵗʰ

Our most intimate relationships can bring us more joy and more suffering than anything else. A relationship is like a mirror. We can better see ourselves and discover who we really are. When we are alone we can enjoy our fantasies, ego trips, and mental games without a problem. But when we try those same things with our partner, the mirror will reflect and will sometime show us our ugly ego trips. A mirror is neutral. It just reflects. It doesn't take sides. In this mirror we can see our tendencies, our weaknesses, and our strengths. The mirror of relationships becomes a good teacher for us to discover who we really are and where we are on our spiritual path.

Paraphrased from the writings of Dzogchen Ponlop Rinpochesd

August 7ᵗʰ

Take a piece of paper and at the top write, "I love myself, therefore ..." Finish this sentence in as many ways as you can. Read it over daily, and add to it as you think of new things. The biggest benefit of doing this exercise is that you learn it is almost impossible to belittle yourself when you say you love yourself. Visualize or imagine yourself having or doing or being what you are working toward. The more you learn and understand yourself, the better you will feel. You are different from everyone else, yet you are a child of God and therefore worthy to be loved.

Paraphrased from the writings of Louise L. Hay

August 8th

Some people spend entirely too much time looking at the actions of others. They compare themselves with other people to judge how they may be
doing themselves. Always remember that first and
foremost, your actions and words should please the
Creator. Secondly, they should please you. If you
can satisfy the Creator and yourself, then you don't
have to worry so much about what other people
think or do. Don't waste your time trying to conform to society and its social dictates. What great
person in history do you know who conformed to
what society expected? The people who've made
a significant contribution to the world walk to
the beat of their own drum. Those who strive too
much to conform are generally insecure and weak.
You should learn who you are. Then be proud of
yourself and go about your life striving to be the
person that the Creator has made.

August 9th

1. Aware of the suffering caused by the destruction of life, I vow to cultivate compassion and learn ways to respect and protect others and never condone the act of killing another person.

2. Aware of the suffering caused by exploitation, I vow to practice generosity by sharing my time, energy, and material resources with those in need.

3. Aware of the suffering caused by sexual misconduct, I am determined not to engage in sexual relations without love and a long-term commitment.

4. Aware of the suffering caused by what I say and my failure to listen, I vow to cultivate loving speech and deep listening in order to bring joy and happiness to others.

5. Aware of the suffering caused by uncontrolled consumption, I vow to cultivate good health by practicing mindful eating, drinking, and proper exercise. I vow to eat only things that bring about peace, well-being, and joy in my body.

Paraphrased from the writings of Thich Nhat Hanh

August 10th

People seem to be dependent on what happens in their life for their happiness. Unhappiness is a disease on our planet. And it's not just in places where people don't have enough. It's even more so where people have more than they need. The affluent world is sometimes lost in content and trapped in ego. People look at the present as being scarred by something terrible that has happened that shouldn't have happened or by something that should've happened that didn't. But what you must realize is that there is perfection that is always here that lies beneath all that is happening in the outside world. You should accept the present moment and find that perfection that is deeper than anything else and untouched by time. The joy of being comes from within you, your spirit, and the Creator that knows that all things that happen are for the ultimate good of mankind.

Paraphrased from the writings of Eckhart Tolle

August 11th

None of us can live independently without relying on other people. When you walk into a store and buy a loaf of bread, you may feel totally disconnected with the clerk, the store owner, the shelf stocker, the trucker, and the farmer who planted the seed. But without all of them, you couldn't have bought that loaf of bread at the store. We need to always be aware of our close relationship and interconnection with other human beings. People may have a different skin color and may talk differently than you, but you must realize that they have an importance in your life. Respect others for what they do and the good works they perform. For all you know, you may be interconnected with them in one way or another.

Paraphrased from the writings of Dzogchen Ponlop Rinpoche

August 12th

Spirituality means the ability to find peace and happiness in an imperfect world. It means to feel that one's own personality is imperfect but acceptable. From this peaceful state of mind come both creativity and the ability to love unselfishly, which go hand in hand. Acceptance, faith, forgiveness, peace, and love are the traits that define spirituality. These characteristics always appear in those who achieve unexpected healing of a serious illness. A person who believes in a benevolent higher power has a potent reason for hope, and hope is the key ingredient in healing.

Paraphrased from the writings of Bernie S. Siegel, M.D.

August 13th

Whenever you go to a buffet, you'll find a large variety of foods spread out for your consumption. How do you go about choosing what to put on your plate? There are foods that are good for you and will make your body healthier. There are foods that are not good for your body and can make your body unhealthy. You may feel frustrated because it's all so enticing. Which voice do you listen to? This analogy is the same that you have with your life. You have choices—things that are good for you and things that are not. Which do you choose? Temptation comes to everyone to do things that are not in their best interest. But if you truly want to pursue a spiritual life and do the right thing, go inside yourself and listen to your inner voice and be guided in making your decisions about what to do with your life.

August 14th

Many people seem to be totally preoccupied with themselves. Some say that self-centeredness can be construed as a longing or a search for fulfillment. These self-absorbed people can't seem to do good deeds for others because they can't get out of themselves. The Christian says that you must first lose yourself in order to find yourself. The Buddhist says that in order to learn about yourself and who you are, you must first forget about yourself and who you are. Confucius said, "In vain I have searched to find a single person capable of seeing clearly his or her own faults." You can never be on a spiritual path as long as you're wrapped up in yourself. Try to remember and make it your mantra: "It's not all about me." You'll find that it's infinitely more rewarding to do good deeds for others than it is to do good deeds for yourself.

Paraphrased from the writings of Daniel Yankelovich

August 15ᵗʰ

If the veil could be drawn aside from where you are, you would be thankful to know that your spiritual companions are there beside you. Try to sense the comfort of their presence, knowing that they have a complete understanding of what is going on in your life. Your guides know your innermost needs and will comfort you when you seek them. It's your love, your belief in love itself that creates the bridge between you and your guides. And the more you love, the more you will be aware of their presence.

Paraphrased from the writings of White Eagle

August 16ᵗʰ

Does it matter what we read or what we watch on TV or what movies we see? Do the people with whom we associate influence our lives? Does our daily routine make a difference? The answer to these questions is, "Undoubtedly, yes." Each action in our lives, no matter how small, has an effect, which is cumulative. With single drops of water, a bucket is filled. So we need to pay attention to what kind of mental habitat we wish to create. We are, in effect, constructing ourselves with each drop of water added to the bucket. An accumulation of undesirable drops could drive us into an activity we might not be happy about later. Although we might not see the effects of it right away, what enters our minds definitely has an influence on our lives. You should make an effort to surround yourself with positive thoughts and actions.

Paraphrased from the writings of Diana Winston

August 17ᵗʰ

In some Asian countries, there's an effective trap they use to catch a monkey. They slit open a coconut wide enough for the monkey to slip its hand in. They secure the coconut to the ground and put a piece of candy inside. The monkey is lured by the smell of the sweet, slips its hand in, and grabs the candy. The monkey could get its hand out if it would only turn the candy loose, but it won't do it. So it gets caught every time. How are you doing in letting go of bad habits and things that are not good for you? Are you trapped by desires like the monkey? To rid yourself of bad habits, you must have strength and self-discipline. To achieve this you must surrender to the Higher Power and let go of your ego and desires. Remember that you give it all up in order to gain it all.

August 18ᵗʰ

It seems that most people live life as if they're driving a car at night. They can never see further than their headlights. No doubt, you can make your entire trip that way. However, some people seem to stay in the dark all the time because they can't see anything except what's right in front of them. Think how much more pleasant it is to drive in the daytime. You can see the whole picture, or at least as far as you're able to see in all directions. That's what enlightenment brings to your life–the difference between driving at night and driving in the daytime. That's why it's so important in your life to pursue enlightenment. If you're not doing it, start today.

Paraphrased from the writings of Rob Brezsny

August 19th

If you do wrong or have ill feelings toward another person then it's like a boomerang. It comes back and hurts you worse than it does them. If you dislike another person, it's really yourself you dislike. The thing you hate the worst in others is always the thing you hate most about yourself. Harboring ill feelings toward others is like a cancer, for it eats away at your soul and gnaws at your inner being. You must let go of your resentments and make yourself right with those you have wronged. Then you must forgive not only others but yourself. Amends to others are important. Amends to yourself are essential!

Paraphrased from the writings of Little Star, Shawnee Tribe

August 20th

A rich man went into the town square where a
famous guru was teaching. He was so moved by
the guru's words that he asked him to come to his
home for dinner. The guru accepted. The rich man
summoned his servants to prepare a banquet with
the best foods they could find. The table was spread
with delicacies fit for a king. That evening, as he
waited for the guru's arrival, there was a knock at
the door. He hurriedly opened it to find only a poor
beggar wanting food. The rich man said, "Go away.
I have an appointment with an important person.
I don't have time for someone like you." So the
beggar left. The rich man waited and waited, but
the guru never came. Disappointed, he went to
the town square the next day and found the guru.
"I had a wonderful meal prepared for you, but
you never came." The guru said, "But I did come
dressed as a beggar, and you turned me away."

August 21ˢᵗ

Believe in yourself. Have confidence in your own powers. With good self-confidence you can succeed in life. Any sense of inferiority and inadequacy interferes with the attainment of your hopes. A faith in a Higher Power can strengthen you and give you the confidence to do the things you want to do. With faith, good things seem to flow toward you rather than away from you.

"If you have faith, nothing shall be impossible to you." (Matthew 17:20)

"If God be for us, who can be against us?" (Romans 8:31)

Paraphrased from the writings of Norman Vincent Peale

August 22nd

Why is it that the white man will cut down a tree and never say the proper prayers? A tree must be asked if it is willing to be cut. You can't just take a tree for granted. Prayers must be said in asking the tree to sacrifice its life for the purpose you need it for. Also, gifts must be given to Grandmother Earth for the gift she has given us. To cut a tree without doing this is like murder. Why doesn't the white man have more respect for nature? Trees are living a life just like we are. God created the trees, and they must be respected. The white man seems to run roughshod over the earth, taking from it whatever he needs for his own use without appreciating it for what it is. They shouldn't take what is growing in nature for granted.

Paraphrased from the writings of Franklin Kahn, Navajo Elder

August 23rd

The spiritual world is waiting for you to connect. Come to terms with it, and surrender to the Creator. Do you complain a lot about what's happening to you? Do you often try to justify things you do? Do you ever blame others for the conditions in your life? Do you often feel guilty about what you say and do? Do you get angry about what someone says? If these ring true to you, then you're not on the path. You're like a lamp that has never been plugged in. What happens when you plug in a lamp and turn it on? Light appears out of darkness. Accept the fact that you're divine and a child of God. You have an abundance of beauty inside you waiting to be tapped. Your life could be so pleasant and happy if you'd just get out of the way and let it happen.

August 24ᵗʰ

You pray earnestly for all your problems to be removed. You long for peace and prosperity and an easy life. But can't you see that it is only by going through the discipline from the problems you face that your eyes are opened? Your spiritual journey requires you to pass through this process of discipline. Therefore, be thankful for your tests and your heartaches. Once your lessons are learned, you will then be able to comprehend and absorb the beauty of the heavenly life.

Paraphrased from the writings of White Eagle

August 25th

We always stop by this place when we drive by where over 400 of our people were driven off the side of a cliff to their deaths—mostly women, children, and old people. That was during the eighteen hundreds when the European settlers came to take over our country where we'd lived for 50,000 years. Sometimes at night when we stand on the side of this cliff, we can hear weeping, moans, and screaming. We always cry for our people who couldn't understand why someone would be so cruel. We hope that people around the world have learned by now that this is not the way to treat others. Yet we read about things every day giving examples of man's inhumanity against others. Only when we feel the grief of what we do to one another will there be change. We'll then see the big picture, and maybe we can learn to live in peace.

Paraphrased from the writings of Faith and Lorraine, Australian Aboriginal Elders

August 26ᵗʰ

If God grants me more of life, I plan to use it to the best of my ability. I'll be more thoughtful of all I say. I'll sleep less and dream more. I'll love more, since people grow old when they stop loving. I'll give wings to children but leave it to them to learn how to fly by themselves. I've learned that everybody wants to live on top of the mountain without knowing that true happiness is obtained in the journey taken to reach the top. I have learned that a man has the right and obligation to look down at another, only when that man needs help to get up from the ground. Say always what you feel, not what you think. Keep your loved ones near you and continually tell them how much you love them.

Gabriel Garcia Marquez, winner of the Nobel Prize for Literature, (written while dying with terminal cancer)

August 27ᵗʰ

You should practice being aware of your breath several times during the day. The more you do it, the deeper your breath will become. Becoming aware of your breath forces you into the present moment, which is the key to all inner transformation. You cannot think and be aware of your breathing at the same time. Without these gaps, your shallow breaths make thinking become repetitive, uninspired, and devoid of any creative spark. When you practice deep breathing, don't feel that you are not thinking but actually rising above thinking. Not only will you come fully into the present moment with deep breathing, but you also are rising into a more spiritual consciousness.

Paraphrased from the writings of Eckhart Tolle

August 28ᵗʰ

Do you find yourself concentrating on a particular thing more often than you should? The more attention you give to a subject the more powerful it becomes. The more you think about it the more it begins to dominate the experiences of your daily life. If the subject matter is not a positive one that is in your best interest then it's like conducting a negative workshop for your mind. So when you catch yourself concentrating too much on negative emotions try to change your thought patterns to things you'd like to experience that are good for you. Little by little you'll change your habit and reverse your negative thoughts to positive ones. Focus more on what you'd like for your life to be like rather than what you don't like about your life.

August 29ᵗʰ

BE MORE LIKE A TREE

Have good, strong roots;

Reach down as well as up;

Stand tall, but bend when you need to;

Be a shelter to someone;

Welcome rainy days;

Know that being beautiful is the same thing as being yourself;

Reach out for the light;

Release to others the light you've found;

Respect your elders;

Make fresh air and not hot air;

Realize that the brightest blossoms are not always on the tallest trees;

Don't let things eat away at you;

Appreciate all the others around you;

Big trees were once little trees that kept growing;

Give of your fruits freely to others;

Your work is to grow;

All trees will one day fall; but life doesn't end, for the fallen tree keeps giving to all that grows around it.

Douglas Wood

August 30th

It's not unusual for humans to judge in haste the actions of others. There are some who are ready to condemn other people for what they think they've done without knowing all the facts. Don't do this, for it brings you down on a lower level. Treat uncomplimentary news about others in a spiritual way by maintaining love in your heart for them. Practice withholding your judgments and criticisms and negative thinking, both in your thoughts and your words. Remember that while you are here on this earth, you are divine as well as human. Try to move beyond the human or lower side of yourself and begin treating things that happen in your life with your spiritual side–the side of love, compassion, and understanding.

Paraphrased from the writings of White Eagle

August 31st

Accept who you are by looking in the mirror and realizing that you are not your body but a Divine Creation. If you can observe everything that occurs in your life without judgment or emotion, then you will see your experiences clearly. Release the things that happen every day in your life and allow yourself to be free. Releasing is having no expectations of outcome and living in the present. Breathe deeply and consciously with thankfulness for the life you've been given.

Paraphrased from the writings of Kara Smith and Ornesha de Paoli

September 1ˢᵗ

Are there things about your life that are not good for you? Things that are holding you back in pursuit of your spiritual path.? Are you aware that you may be undergoing a certain amount of emotional pain and suffering because of these conditions in your life that you've continued to cling to? In order to make progress, you must make changes. If you're willing to renounce those things that are dragging you down, you will begin receiving fresh opportunities and much greater blessings. You've been given this life with countless opportunities. So examine yourself. If changes need to be made to make you a happier more productive person, then don't waste another day. Life is too precious to let slip by. Don't squander any more time. Do it now!

Paraphrased from the writings of White Eagle

September 2nd

Our grandparents and parents were told that the new technology would give them so much more leisure time to do what they'd like. What happened? We have had an abundance of new technology over the past generation, but we seem to have less leisure time than our forebears. We need to pay more attention to each thing that happens in our life and not keep our minds on what's going to happen next. Being in the present with each moment of life is the way to live life more spiritually.

Paraphrased from the writings of Helena Norberg-Hodge

September 3rd

For some people, being sick strengthens their ego. They get a great deal of pleasure telling others about their illness because it makes others feel sorry for them. That's ego in its purest form. It not only burns up a considerable amount of energy, but it also takes much longer for them to recover. On the other hand, there are others who become more humble during an illness. They, very often, gain much insight they'd never had before. Their illness teaches them not to take things for granted and to be more appreciative of good health. They use their illness as a stepping stone toward humility. These people have a much better recovery rate and even find it helpful in their spiritual growth.

Paraphrased from the writings of Eckhart Tolle

September 4th

Now that I'm ninety years old, I've been looking back over my life. I've always been one of those people who lived sensibly and predictably hour after hour, day after day. If I had my life to live over again, I'd relax more, limber up, and act sillier. I'd take more chances and not take things so seriously. I'd climb more mountains and swim more rivers in the nude. I'd eat more ice cream and fewer beans. I'd go to more dances and ride more merry-go-rounds. I'd find more things to laugh at and fewer things to worry about. I may have just as many troubles, but I'd have a whole lot less imaginary ones.

Paraphrased from the writings of Nadine Stair, Louisville, Kentucky

September 5th

A child's world is fresh and new and beautiful, full of wonder and excitement. Unfortunately, as we grow older what is fresh and new and beautiful is dimmed or even lost in the world of being an adult. If there were just some way we could keep that child-like excitement about things as we grow older. Truthfully, there is a way to avoid the cynicism of adulthood—if you believe and have faith that there is a Greater Power that knows all and guides us along the way. That it's all good, no matter how bad it may seem. Then you can have a world that is exciting and beautiful and full of wonder.

Paraphrased from the writings of Rachel Carson

September 6th

We are all very much a part of nature. Trees and rivers have the right to exist and perform their normal function. The coyote has the right to howl. The earth needs to be liberated from the plan of humans to continually develop and expand and, in the process, destroy nature.

Paraphrased from the writings of Gary Snyder

September 7th

"The American Dream" is to have lots of money, loads of material possessions, and good social standing. Children are given things and told they belong only to them, not their brother or sister or friend. It's theirs to keep. Early on, they learn to have attachments to their possessions and will fight to keep them. The children of Native Americans and other indigenous tribes, on the other hand, have been taught to give to another the thing they treasure most. They believe that a system of hoarding possessions disturbs one's spiritual balance by placing too much emphasis on materialism. Not a single tangible thing you own is worth more than your relationship to the Creator. Prove it to yourself by giving away something you prize. If someone compliments you on something you're wearing, give it to them. It will teach you to put less stock in material things, thus moving you forward on your spiritual path.

September 8th

It's perfectly natural to be drawn to people whom you like and to ignore people you don't. That's human nature. But has it ever occurred to you that this trait may be a weakness in you? The Creator dwells within every person, no matter how he or she may appear on the surface. It's only your separation from the Creator that makes you ignore those people who seem so different. All people can go down into the center of their being in order to reunite with the Creator at any time. Everyone has that capability. But you can never attain enlightenment until you can see the Creator within all people regardless of how they may appear on the outside.

Paraphrased from the writings of Edgar Cayce

September 9th

What good does it do to get angry? It's such a waste of good energy. Often getting angry is a refusal to see life in a new and different way. Could it be possible that you are creating situations to get angry at? Are you giving out energy that attracts in others the need to irritate you? Why do you believe that to get your way you need to be angry? In the infinity of life, all is perfect, whole, and complete. Look closely at the patterns of your life and be willing to make changes. Be willing to release certain fixed ideas of always having to have things your own way. If you will discard the unimportant things in your life, you can learn to be free. And all will be well in your world.

Paraphrased from the writings of Louise L. Hay

September 10th

The way you feel about yourself is a strong and powerful tool. Your thoughts send messages to your body, and your body reacts to this communication. If your mind is sending thoughts of illness to your body, it will respond likewise. If you send positive thoughts of wellness to your body, it can become a powerful healing technique. This also works with the message "I am a happy person" or "I am a sad or depressed person." If you feel poor, you can't attract prosperity. If you feel fat, you cannot attract thin. If you feel that your unfortunate condition, whatever it may be, is unchangeable, then you will maintain the status quo. Try concentrating on a vision of happiness for yourself. See yourself as a happy person each time you look in the mirror. By all means, look upon yourself as a good person, who is worthy of being loved.

Paraphrased from the writings of Esther and Jerry Hicks

September 11ᵗʰ

Your life can be greatly enhanced by the power of positive affirmation. By using this tool, you can awaken a state of awareness that allows you to see things unfolding in a positive way rather than a negative one. When you speak and think in an affirmative way it will change how you view yourself, your relationship with others, as well as your relationship with God. Since you are a spiritual being, you have that source available to you at any time to view things in a positive way. By living your life in a positive manner, you will strengthen yourself and energize your mind. Living your life in a positive way will make you more goal-oriented, giving you the power to fulfill your desires.

Paraphrased from the writings of Roy Eugene Davis

September 12th

The things that hurt you the most are your most powerful teachers. You are here on this earth to experience reality, not just hear about it or watch it pass by. If you are holding onto pain, you need to let it go. Holding onto pain means that you're living in the past. Remember that love can only be experienced in the present. Sometimes people don't let go of pain because it leaves behind shame, guilt, and fear. These emotions are really pain in disguise. When you release yourself from the shackles of pain, you will clear your heart for the presence of love.

Paraphrased from the writings of Robert P. Jocoby

September 13ᵗʰ

To understand who we really are, we must understand the meaning of silence. Within silence there is balance. Mind and body become transparent, and we can discover who we really are. When everything becomes simplified through silence, all the tangles of our inner knots and problems gradually dissolve. True silence comes from within. Silence is not merely the absence of speech. It is pure naturalness, absolute calm, without fixation, without preparation. Nothing is required except, simply, to be.

Paraphrased from the writings of Tarthang Tulku

September 14th

Your body is a temple that houses your spirit. While it's more important to stay in touch with the spiritual side, you should never neglect the body. Treat it with the respect it deserves, for the body is a holy place.

1. It's important to eat healthy food, only occasionally splurging on things you crave that aren't particularly good for you.
2. Drink lots of water. The body wants it and needs it.
3. If you drink alcohol, do it in moderation.
4. It's good to work, but don't become a workaholic.
5. Physical exercise is necessary to keep the body in shape and prevent being overweight.
6. In all of this, moderation is the key.
7. If you do all these things, don't be self-righteous about it. This has a tendency to make you tense and uptight.

Try to live your life with love in your heart for others, and treat you body with the self-respect it deserves.

September 15ᵗʰ

Don't ever have the victim mentality by saying there are forces out there you can't control and you're at the mercy of your upbringing, your lack of education, your parents, your spouse and family, your boss, the economy, the politicians, large corporations, or the rich, or some particular enemy who is out to get you. If you believe that this discharges you from any responsibility for your life and it's not your fault then you're dead wrong. True, we're at the mercy of some things we have no control over. But there's a vast difference between being a victim and having the victim mentality. You have more control over your life than you may think. Give life every ounce of strength to try to make things happen in your best interest. If you've given 110 percent toward a project or idea or relationship and it doesn't work then you must release it. Don't be attached to it and always accept the hand you've been dealt.

Paraphrased from the writings of Richard Bolles

September 16th

HEALING

1. Love and laughter are the greatest physicians of the universe with the power to heal.
2. If you're in conflict with your illness, chances are that healing will not occur. Submit to the healing process.
3. Don't judge others as bad or good. Accept them as they are.
4. Forgiveness is the key to happiness. Surrender all judgment of self and others and allow the healing power of inner serenity to manifest.
5. Free yourself of attachments to your possessions and your pride, and let go of the principle cause of stress in your life.
6. Faith is a deep intuitive knowledge that a higher spiritual power is at work in your life. Surrender to it and let a great burden be lifted.
7. Hope is an attitude of positive expectancy that enhances the will to live and boosts the immune system.

8. Help others and quit focusing on your own problems.

Paraphrased from the writings of Dr. Raymond Moody, M.D.

September 17th

Do you sometimes find yourself jumping from one thing to another without doing a worthwhile job on any of them? Don't spread yourself too thin—learn to say no. Pick and choose those things that are important to you, and then give them your very best shot. If you have too many irons in the fire, you wind up chasing your tail and don't get any satisfaction from any of them. Gandhi said, "It doesn't matter what your job is, even if it's scrubbing toilets; but whatever it is, take pride in doing the best job you can in everything you undertake." The old saying that you get out of something what you put into it is really very true. As you go about your day, be selective in what you choose to do. Then give your very best effort to those things that you've selected.

September 18th

We must be willing to change our ways. We can no longer be content to say, "I'm only human." We must recognize that we are also divine. We must pray for our enemies, for those who dislike us, and for those we dislike. We must make every effort to see God in each other by looking past the outer façade and seeing a soul there. We must reach out for the spiritual forces who are our guides. We must sound the note of unity within diversity and have respect for all. We must be honest and fulfill the highest we know we are capable of. As Gandhi said, "Be the change you want to see happen in the world."

Paraphrased from the writings of Susan A. Lendvay

September 19th

You must realize that all of creation loves you very much. Even now, your guardian angels are cooking up mysteries that will excite you. They are collaborating to make sure you have all you need in order to make your next move. Are you willing to start loving life back with an equal intensity of the love that is being bestowed upon you? There is plenty of room for you to demonstrate. While life is showering you with blessings, the least you could do is to assist in doling out blessings to help everyone else get what they need. Recognize the truth about the people you care about. Realize that they embody the beauty that is being showered upon them, yet they, like you, also fall short of embodying that beauty. Try to make them feel appreciated and inspire them to do what they can to help others.

Paraphrased from the writings of Rob Brezsny

September 20th

Life is short. Some say that life is as fleeting as a house on fire. When you're young, it seems time lasts forever. As you grow older, it flies by. Have you noticed when you're on vacation in a place far away you try to make the most of your time by doing and seeing the main attractions? Start now by thinking of your life as though you were on a vacation and you have no idea when you're going to have to board the plane to fly back home. Auntie Mame said, "Life is a banquet, and most poor fools are starving to death." Get your priorities straight by being more selective in how you spend your time. Never has a dying person said, "I wish I'd spent more time working at the office." Spend more time with your family, your loved ones, and do more things you enjoy doing. Your life will be enriched by making these changes.

September 21st

Some believe that success comes from using their ambition and greed to get what they want and make things go their way. Yet we know that true success is having a fulfilled, meaningful, and happy mind. But how? First, you must go into a quiet place and learn how your mind works. Meditation will give you the opportunity to observe the movement of your mind. Watch it jump about from one thought to another. Then eliminate thoughts of yourself, and you'll lay the foundation for a shift in attitude. While in meditation, wish happiness for all those you love. But, more importantly, wish happiness for those you dislike the most. Giving them love will cause your mind to be at ease. Love really means wanting others to experience happiness without suffering. Don't concentrate so much on yourself. Extend yourself out to others. Doing so will not only bring you success but will also make your life much more meaningful.

Paraphrased from the writings of Sakyong Mipham Rinpoche

September 22nd

Life should be lived with a good attitude and a thankful spirit. Get into a habit of saying many times during the day to the Creator, "Thank you for my life." Don't take things for granted. Feel appreciative for everything you've been given. As strange as it may seem, you should also give thanks for the unpleasant things that happen to you. Those are the things that teach you valuable lessons and give you strength to carry on with your life. Make an effort to look at the positive things in your life instead of the negative ones. Being always thankful will make you better able to meet life every day with enthusiasm. This type of attitude will take you a long way in having a more enjoyable, productive life.

September 23rd

It is slow and tedious work for God to make a man and a woman into His own image. The only way for us to ever be useful is to allow God to take us through the crooks and crannies of our own characters in order to learn who we really are. It is astounding how ignorant we are about ourselves! We don't seem to know envy or laziness or pride when we see it. Most people don't understand themselves and how their lives are driven by their egos, the greatest curse in the spiritual life. You cannot be on your spiritual path until you have gotten rid of your ego and become humble and contrite. Know that you don't know. Open your mind and be receptive as a small child. Then you can learn more about whom you really are and where you fit into the Divine Plan.

Paraphrased from the writings of Oswald Chambers

September 24th

It's so essential to the health of your mind and body to have a good sense of humor. If you were to count the number of times each day you laugh aloud, how many would it be? It should be a lot. Stress, worry, and anxiety bring about a world of problems for your mind and body to deal with. If you allow yourself to be overcome with problems, they will consume you. Stress will bring about illness and disease, so work on bringing more joy into your life. They say that laughter is the best medicine that you can take. In order to overcome all the stress, worry, anxiety, and downright sadness you may have, it's necessary to have the help and guidance of a Higher Power. Pray, meditate, read inspiring words, talk to people you respect, and then give it all up to the Higher Power. Then you'll become more carefree, joyful, and happy.

September 25ᵗʰ

Rejoice in the abundance of being able to awaken each morning and experience a new day. Be glad and thankful that you're alive, that you have the strength to perform your daily routine, and that you have family and friends. Having received these gifts, learn to be creative and be a living example of the joy of being alive. Live to your highest potential. Enjoy your transformational process through this lifetime and into the next.

Paraphrased from the writings of Louise L. Hay

September 26th

Every once in awhile you should sit down and take stock of yourself. Don't just look at the immediate or what's happening presently in your life. Put your whole life in perspective. How does it shape up? What is your focus in life? What do you want your future to be like? All of your possessions are temporary. Your body that you spend so much time and money on is temporary. In fact, there's only one thing you possess that's permanent, and that's your spirit. Do you feel that most of your waking hours are spent on the temporary and very few, if any, spent on what's permanent? Start now by getting in touch with your spirit. Go deep inside in meditation, commune with the spirit, then surrender every temporary thing you have–your possessions, your mind, your heart, your body, and your spirit to God.

September 27th

Go about your daily work with a spirit of goodness and love in your heart. Don't think of your work as a job or a task but more as a service to others, as well as to yourself. Tend to the ordinary details of your life as if they were sacred. Without imagination for the sacred in our everyday experiences, we are destined for a life without soul. Soul and the sacred go together. If you bring this spirit into everything you do, it will enhance your life and bring about an abundance of happiness.

Paraphrased from the writings of Thomas Moore

September 28th

The Creator gave you a mind to think and make decisions and also endowed you with a spirit that lives within. You have been told that "the kingdom of heaven is within." Most times, however, you use your mortal mind rather than your spirit to think and make decisions. You must remember that the mortal mind can be fallible. It can't be completely trusted, whereas the spirit world that lives within you is perfect. While you continually seek help from outside sources, the true answers to your problems come from within. The spirit world that brings peace out of chaos lives deep within if you. All you need to do is search for it. As you go about your daily activities, remember the resource that you have available inside you to make your important decisions. Try to be more spiritual and less mortal.

September 29ᵗʰ

You can never progress along the spiritual path so long as you are wrapped up in your own ego. You must get beyond it. But some people make the mistake of moving from their personal ego by identifying with a group. It may be patriotism toward your country. It could be identifying with a particular political party. You may become involved in a church, a club, a gang, a football team, or many other groups. There's nothing wrong with any of these organizations so long as you have not shifted your ego from the personal to the collective. Some of those groups can develop a need to conflict with others. They need to feel that they're right and others are wrong—just as some nations sometimes engage in behavior that would be defined as psychopathic if it were an individual. On your spiritual journey, you will only progress if you move beyond both the personal and the collective ego.

Paraphrased from the writings of Eckhart Tolle

September 30th

If you want to progress spiritually, it's essential that you respect all forms of life—not just people but animals and all living creatures. You can't move in the right direction and have ill will toward any other person. Ill will toward another creates a polarization in your life that's neither healthy nor good. You can't just be nice to the people who are like you and agree with you. Remember it was Jesus who said that it's easy to be friendly and nice to your friends, but you get no points for that. To befriend the person you dislike or the one who dislikes you is the foundation not only of the Christian religion but almost all other religions as well. The next time you enter your church or mosque or synagogue or temple, believe in your heart that it's not just those who are like you who are worthy but those of all religions and nationalities who deserve your love and respect also.

October 1st

Interaction with other people can sometimes get complicated. When another person does something that irritates you, don't get all upset at the injustice of it all. It's natural for humans to place blame on others for wrong-doing. If you want to be on the spiritual path, you cannot attack another person, even in your thoughts. Turning the other cheek is sometimes difficult. But if you wish to progress spiritually and move forward into the light, there can be no compromise, no excuses. You must treat everyone, including the person who has offended you, with love, gentleness, and peace. The offending party will receive his or her judgment in due time. It's not up to you to right the wrongs of the world. Leave it alone and let it go. We have no understanding of how the Creator works. However, those on the spiritual path know that what happens is to our overall advantage.

October 2nd

It is said that some newborns come into the world with a heavy share of emotional pain. As they grow, so does their body pain. It may seem contradictory, but these people seem to have a better chance of awakening spiritually. Being unable to live with their unhappiness, they become motivated to awaken and become strong. However, if they don't seek the spiritual route, they can become addicted to their unhappiness. They not only refuse to end their pain, but they also want others to feel as miserable as they do. These people feed on drama, discord, and unhappiness and are attracted to others who feel the same way. Egos love things such as this. If you are one of these people, you need to begin working on allowing yourself to become vast, spacious, and whole. By doing this, your true nature will emerge, allowing you to become one with God.

Paraphrased from the writings of Eckhart Tolle

October 3rd

The key to solving most of life's problems lies in attempting to understand our mind. The mind's natural condition is a state of open awareness. Through meditation we can connect with this openness, rid our minds of negative judgments, and free ourselves from anger, frustration, and pain. Meditation allows us to let go of fear and anxiety, be more honest and compassionate, and become more focused and relaxed. When we are able to still our body, breath, and mind, a very comfortable, soothing feeling naturally arises. During meditation don't try to interpret your feelings intellectually, for the thought process itself separates us from the experience. When we don't allow our minds to fill with thoughts, negative forces will have nothing to grasp and so they cannot be of harm to us.

Paraphrased from the writings of Tarthang Tulku

October 4ᵗʰ

It's essential to manage your thoughts and keep
your mind focused in the right direction. In connection with that, you must control your wants
and desires. Always wanting something new is
a sure sign of unhappiness. It's alright to occasionally have new things, but some people have
an obsession with their desires for material goods
that keeps them chasing their tails all the time.
Controlling your desires promotes contentment
and increases your capacity for doing more good
works for others. That's where your focus should
be. When the opportunity presents itself, jump at
the chance to do something helpful for other people. Living a moral life is essential for any person on the spiritual path. And in order to observe
morality you must attain a mastery over your mind
and your passions. When you do that, you'll find
that you will begin to learn who you really are.

October 5th

Your sole purpose in life is to strive to be a conduit for God on earth. In order to do this, you must surrender your ego and give it all up to God. Offer no resistance and let God come into your life. By ridding yourself of all the pride and ego which stand in your way, you'll be able to allow God's Love, Light, and Holy Spirit to flow through you and out to others. Once you do this, you'll realize that this is your true purpose in life.

Paraphrased from the writings of K.J. Stewart

October 6th

If you started yelling at a child, telling him how stupid he is, you'd end up with a frightened child who does nothing or who, in anger, tries to tear up the place. You'd never know the potential of that child because he would have gone off in the wrong direction. But take the same child and tell him how much you love him, how you care, that you love the way he looks, that it's okay to make mistakes, and that you'll always be there for him, and the potential of that child is unlimited. The same applies to the way you treat yourself. It's easy to blame parents, be a victim for the rest of your life, and beat up on yourself, but you don't have to do that. Give yourself love and praise, tell yourself that it's okay to make mistakes, and that the Creator loves you. It will make a difference in your life.

Paraphrased from the writings of Louise L. Hay

October 7th

If you find that you no longer crave the stimulus of adrenalin-driven entertainment and have more of a desire to enjoy simple things like listening to the sound of rain or wind, seeing the beauty of clouds, being in a tranquil setting in nature, or treating a complete stranger with heartfelt kindness without expecting anything in return, then this means a space is being opened up in your stream of thinking. When this happens, you will gain a sense of well-being, of peace, and a desire for calm. This can only come, however, for those who have a desire for contentment, peace, and aliveness. It's difficult to find that sense of peace and contentment in a busy world like ours, but it can be done by becoming conscious of being conscious. In a quiet place, say or think the words "I am" and add nothing to it—then be aware of the stillness that follows.

October 8th

We have to realize that nothing is permanent. Yet impermanence not only controls our lives, it holds sway over the entire universe. From history, we see the rise and fall of nations, and even heavenly bodies are not permanent. While impermanence permeates all existence, we still seem to hold on to the idea of permanence in our lives. But impermanence is a part of being alive. To be born a human is a very rare privilege. It is important that we appreciate our lives and take advantage of this opportunity for human existence. Accepting impermanence as a part of our life is necessary to make our lives more satisfying. We can then more easily let go of our attachments and fears, as well as our shell of protection. This letting go of what we believe to be permanent will help to wake us up and realize that at this very moment we are actually alive!

Paraphrased from the writings of Tarthang Tulku

October 9th

There once was a seeker, who searched the world over for the truth. Then one day, as he was sitting on a mountaintop, he saw a light, a blinding sheet of white light. But the light was not coming from the sun, it came from within him. The light spread into an ever-widening circle until it filled the whole universe. Then from the inner vision he heard a voice say, "I am the light—the light which shines within you—the light that fills the world. From me springs all things, all beings, and all universes. I am the living God—the knowledge you seek, the wisdom, the understanding, and love. Your purpose here on this earth is to express love for every living thing, for without love neither you nor I can exist. Without love there would be nothing. All life is united with me by love, for it is only by my love that life exists."

Paraphrased from the writings of Paul Twitchell

October 10th

When you have a scientific world that believes the only reality is what you can grasp with your senses, it makes the material world take on an exaggerated importance, as if it were the only reality. It makes you become a slave to your possessions. In spite of the fact that materialism has become a curse of the western world, people seem to be oblivious to its implications. It should be obvious to all that the material world does not feed the spirit and, in fact, takes away from it. And if we do know it, then why do we continue to grab for more and more material things that will never satisfy us? We need to come to terms with the fact that the only way to find true and lasting satisfaction is from a spiritual life. Let's not allow the disease of materialism to rob us of the happiness we're entitled to.

Paraphrased from the writings of Tatanka Yotanka, Lakota Sioux

October 11th

Most people are so caught up in their daily routines that their lives are deprived of significance. Inwardly, they long for freedom to be who they're meant to be. They have the mistaken belief that prosperity will bring this freedom to them. But those who have prosperity are well aware that this is not enough to fill one's life with meaning. There is no substitute for finding the true purpose of your life, and you can't find this purpose on the outer level. It concerns who you really are and the state of your consciousness. Internally you long to be the person you were destined to be and to fulfill your true purpose in life. To discover your inner being, you must continually go deep within during meditation to your spiritual center. It's so important for you to accomplish this as soon as you can because discovering your inner being and walking on the spiritual path are the only things that will bring you true happiness.

October 12th

Allow yourself to be a being of love and it will replace any fear and unhappiness you may have in your life. Quiet your mind and go inside yourself to realize more of your true nature–your peace. From this place you can observe your mind and your ego. From this place you can learn to love all aspects of yourself. It's the place where you can make decisions that will be best for you instead of letting the ego do it for you. Learn to use the ego as a positive instrument for individual experience in your life instead of allowing it to be a prison of individual bondage.

Paraphrased from the writings of K.J. Stewart

October 13ᵗʰ

Be mindful that when you have a problem, you should not just look at the problem itself. Doing so results in negative emotions. But when you focus on a solution to your problem, you're introducing positive emotions to help solve your problem. Also, be aware of this when you're speaking to loved ones about their illnesses or problems. Try to imagine them as being well and happy instead of focusing on their illness or trouble. When your words focus on their recovery instead of their illness, you're focusing on their well-being. Try to connect your inner being with their inner being. Connecting with your inner being gives you much more power and influence in helping you, as well as your loved ones, to overcome their illnesses and problems.

October 14ᵗʰ

Life can be really very simple. What we give out, we get back. What we think about ourselves becomes the truth for us. We are 100 percent responsible for everything in our lives, the best and the worst. Every thought we think and every feeling we have is creating our future. No person, or place, or anything needs to have any power over us. Most of us have foolish ideas of who we are and many rigid rules about how life should be lived. However, the only thing we're ever dealing with is a thought, and a thought can be changed. Resentment, criticism, guilt, and fear cause more problems than anything else. If we create peace and harmony and balance in our minds, we'll find it in our lives as well. The universe totally supports us in every thought we choose to think and believe along those lines.

Paraphrased from the writings of Louise L. Hay

October 15th

How many times have you heard someone say that they insist on knowing the truth? But to understand the truth, you must have a very sharp, precise, and clear mind. Not a cunning mind, but a mind that is capable of looking at things without any distortion. Obviously, the minds that are most able to do this are those that are innocent and vulnerable. If your mind is crammed full of knowledge, then you'll never be able to perceive what the truth really is. Only a mind that is completely capable of receiving and learning can do that. To be able to learn, you must empty your mind of its accumulation of knowledge and approach the subject with a child-like nature. Then you'll discover that true learning is being able to successfully move from one moment to the next without difficulty. And that can only be done with an open mind.

October 16ᵗʰ

When you breathe in the breath of God, you are breathing in harmony and healing. There is much to learn about the art of breathing, for the way you perform this simple act can affect your whole life—your spiritual unfolding and your physical, mental, and spiritual health. At this moment, relax your mind and body, and breathe deeply, quietly, and slowly. As your breathe in, try to imagine that you are breathing in light and life; that you are not only inhaling air, you are filling every particle of your being with God's breath. As you do this, you will naturally be freed from the problems that constrict you because your whole mind will be focused on God, and it will bring you a sense of peace, poise, and control.

Paraphrased from the prayers and invocations of White Eagle

October 17th

Silence is not just the absence of sound. It's the toning down of inner and outer noise that occupies the ears and the attention. Silence allows many sounds to reach your awareness that would otherwise go unheard. Go out into nature away from all human-made noises. You will begin to hear the sounds of birds, water, wind, trees, frogs, insects, as well as your own conscience, daydreams, intuitions, and wishes. One cultivates silence not by forcing the ears not to hear, but by turning up the volume on the music of the world and the soul.

Paraphrased from the writings of Thomas Moore

October 18th

Remember that your mind and body are in constant communication with each other. However most of this communication is not on a conscious level. What you say to others about your body sends a message to your body, so don't say negative things. The mind should always communicate good thoughts and send positive messages to your body. In your meditation each day, thank your body for serving you and ask it to be well. Tell your immune system to protect you. Visualize your brain, your bones, your liver, your lungs, your heart, and tell them to be free of disease. Always thank God for your body, and then do everything you can on an outward level to make your body healthy. The *Tao Te Ching* says, "Whatever is flexible and flowing will tend to grow, and whatever is rigid and blocked will wither and die."

October 19th

If I've learned anything in my lifelong quest to unravel the mystery of my existence, it is the difference in what I call religion and reality. The God of religion is definable. In reality, there's no such thing as even attempting to define God. When you approach the institutional God, it's like riding in a ship across the ocean. In reality, I've learned that I am the ocean, or, at least, one drop that will return to the ocean upon my death. Every drop that allows itself to fall into the ocean will become the ocean without taking away from the consciousness of any other drop. I've also learned that a Realized Soul will instinctively meditate, express wisdom, and give openheartedly.

Paraphrased from the writings of Vernon Kitabu Turner, Roshi

October 20th

One of the most admirable characteristics about people is humility. No one likes a braggart or someone who is boastful. The people who want to do all the talking are those who don't learn much. Humility is the acceptance of the possibility that someone else can teach you something you don't already know, especially about yourself. So be humble and open to what others have to say. To know that you don't know something is much better than to pretend to know when you don't. Pride and arrogance closes the door of the mind. Practice giving your love to others, make them feel good about themselves, and show your appreciation for the people they are.

October 21ˢᵗ

So many people get caught up in the routine of daily living that their lives are deprived of significance. They long to be free to expand their lives in new and exciting ways. Our society teaches that this can be found by having more money and more prosperity, which will bring about security. But it's only after having it that one realizes this is not enough to fill their life with meaning. The true purpose of life cannot be found in having material things and lots of money, for it concerns who you are, what you are, and your state of consciousness. While everyone needs to have a sufficient amount of income and material things to provide for their basic needs, beyond that the focus should be placed on discovering your inner being, the spiritual side of yourself. That is what brings about true happiness and is the principle that needs to be taught to our children and grandchildren.

Paraphrased from the writings of Eckhart Tolle

October 22ⁿᵈ

Do you feel you are growing more spiritual in your life? You may ask, "How would I know?" The first recognition that your spiritual growth is authentic is when you realize that you're becoming more peaceful and tranquil and accepting of what you've been given. If you continue to get angry, stirred up, impatient, and controlling, then you need to work on some of the following things:

1. Exercise discipline over your thoughts, emotions, and actions.
2. Strive to have a closer relationship with God and a closer relationship with your true nature.
3. Live a natural, wholesome, uncomplicated life and nurture your physical health.
4. Strive to get beyond your ego and practice humility.
5. Cultivate and use your intellectual powers and intuition to determine your true self.

Meditate regularly in order to bring about physical relaxation, mental and emotional calmness, and a clear state of awareness.

October 23rd

All forms of life are interdependent on each other. The prey is as dependent on the predator for control of its population as the predator is on the prey for food. The stability and harmony of the ecosystem are dependent on diversity. One that contains a hundred different species is more stable than one that has only three. All resources such as food, water, air, minerals, and energy are finite. There are limits to the growth of all living systems. These limits are dictated by the finite size of the earth and the finite input of energy from the sun. Our spiritual quest is not only enriched by reverence for the earth, but it is incomplete without it.

Paraphrased from the writings of Vine Deloria

October 24th

We live in a world where bad news is constantly run on television news channels and in the newspapers. It makes it very difficult for the people who watch these news channels on a daily basis to have a positive attitude. How can you be happy and light-hearted when the world is in such turmoil? While you need to know something about what's going on in the world, it's not good for you to get saturated each day with a negative bombardment of information. The power of positive thinking is what you need to enhance your life. If you have faith in God, then you will see things unfolding in a positive rather than a negative light. Because you are a spiritual being, you have that spirit available inside you that allows you to view things in a positive way. Being positive will strengthen and energize your mind and empower you to make progress on your spiritual path.

October 25th

A group of gerontologists conducted an experiment among a number of elderly people who still had their physical and mental faculties. They found that the aging process was greatly accelerated by those who worried excessively about things over which they had no control. Many told of experiencing loneliness with no friends to talk to. Each day was the same. They had no challenges and nothing to be enthused about. Some had financial burdens and not enough money to live on. There were those who regretted how their lives had been lived and wished they could live their lives over. A lot were irritable and became angry very easily. They criticized others and took no responsibility for their own problems. But what these gerontologists found was how their subjects' attitudes changed for the better when they began to focus their time and energy on other people. Helping others and being responsible for others gave them a reason to live.

Paraphrased from the writings of Deepak Chopra

October 26th

"Today, thanks to this rather lopsided cultural foundation, we live in what is commonly described as a 'materialistic society.' But that description is in error. Ours is in reality an 'abstract value society'—one in which things are not appreciated for what they *are* so much as for what they *represent*. If western industrial society appreciated the material world, there would be no junkyards, no clear-cut forests, no shoddily designed and manufactured products, no poisoned water sources, no obese people, fuel-guzzling automobiles, nor any of the other horrors and eyesores that haunt us at every turn. If ours were a materialistic society, we would love the physical world—and we would know our limits within it."

Quote from *The Te of Piglet*, Benjamin Hoff

October 27th

It's not only important for individuals to live a moral life, but also nations must be moral, as well. There can be no legitimate economic policy that ignores or disregards moral values. An economy that enables the strong to amass wealth at the expense of the weak is a false and dismal science. It can only spell death to a society. True economics stands for social justice and promotes the good of all equally, including the very weakest links. We must work for an economy that promotes a decent life for all.

Paraphrased from the writings of Mahatma Gandhi

October 28*th*

It has been said that diseases come to those who are unwilling to forgive. If you're ill, look around to see if there's someone you haven't forgiven. Forgiveness means giving up any ill will toward another. The hardest person to forgive is the one you need to let go of the most. Quit holding on to that unpleasant experience. Forgiveness does not mean condoning what was said or what happened. You may be completely justified in feeling that you're right and the other person was wrong. But that's missing the point. You've got to realize you're not hurting them, you're hurting yourself. Even if you don't know how to forgive, at least be willing to forgive. The universe will take care of the rest. So if you want to maintain good health and avoid illness, let go of every negative thought you have toward others and watch what will take place in your heart, mind, and body.

October 29th

"I like the idea of the eternal self' and taking responsibility for one's life. It comes down to not thinking you gotta do it all right now; and if you don't do it now, you'll never get to do it again because you only live once. If you think you only live once, you're gonna have wars, bank robbers, and greed for money. It makes people not care about anyone else since everybody's in a hurry to have it all right now. When a person gets rich, they don't realize it, but they've only got half of something not the whole. It's no great mystery about why things are the way they are. Things like doubt, denial, fear, and trepidation create artificial barriers from what's real. I believe if we live for an eternity, I'll always be me, and you'll always be you. Life will be like having an eternal adventure. I like that."

Quote by Wayne Shorter, Jazz Saxophonist

October 30*th*

You're aware that in order to be on the spiritual path you must love others and treat them with tolerance and respect. However, it's just as important to love yourself as well. Loving yourself does not mean you should become self-absorbed. It means liking the person you are. The more good things you do for others and the more unselfish you become, the more you'll begin to love yourself. And by loving, accepting, and approving of yourself, it will cause everything in your life to work well. Your health will improve, you'll be more successful in the things you undertake, and your relationships will become more fulfilling. You will express yourself in more creative and fulfilling ways. People who love themselves and their bodies will neither abuse themselves nor anyone else. Never criticize yourself for the things you do. Understand and be gentle with yourself if you really want to improve.

October 31st

Before you can progress on your spiritual journey, one essential ingredient is to love and respect yourself. If you dislike yourself, you'll never make it. So first learn to be a person who is lovable, performs good works for others, and refrains from doing things that make you ashamed of yourself. Once you begin to love and accept and approve of yourself, then everything in life begins to work properly. Your health will improve, your relationship with others becomes more fulfilling, and you will begin expressing yourself in fulfilling ways. Self-approval begins by not criticizing yourself for the things you do. Criticism of yourself locks you into a pattern of negativity that you should avoid. Understanding yourself and being gentle with yourself helps you to move out of this pattern. Start today approving of yourself as a person then sit back and see what happens.

Paraphrased from the writings of Louise L. Hay

November 1st

In Tibetan tradition, it's considered a very rare event for a person to earn the right to be born. An occasion as rare as this is one that is highly prized and celebrated. Tibetans believe that to be born with a human body is to be born with the perfect vehicle for obtaining realization and enlightenment. The body is considered a temple that houses the spirit within. It is not only the reflection or embodiment of the cosmos, but it's also a form of the divine. The body, it is believed, holds the potential of being one of life's greatest teachers. "To keep the body in good health is a duty...otherwise we shall not be able to keep our mind strong and clear," said Buddha.

November 2nd

Proponents of the power of the mind in financial matters tell us that our thinking is the key to creative financing. It is true that our positive belief at the beginning of a doubtful undertaking is the one thing that ensures the successful outcome of the venture. When you expect the best out of yourself, you release a magnetic force in your mind, which by the law of attraction tends to bring the best to you. "As a man thinketh, so is he," says the Holy Bible, Book of Proverbs, chapter 23, verse 7. So many people seek material wealth to make them happy. But true prosperity means that you are receiving peace, good health and enough to satisfy your basic needs. Thinking positive thoughts can make those dreams come true.

"Save and invest as though you would live forever. Share and spend as though you would die tomorrow." Lois Johnstad

November 3rd

When the U.S. went to war against Mexico in 1846, Henry David Thoreau was jailed for refusing to pay his taxes. His friend, Ralph Waldo Emerson, visited him and said, "Henry, what are you doing in there?" He responded, "What are you doing out there?" Thoreau believed that going to war, unless waged clearly in self-defense of the country, was as wrong as murder. He also felt that espousing his religious beliefs was not sufficient. He must act on his beliefs, as well. Likewise, Gandhi said, "Those who think religion and politics are not connected don't know much about politics or religion." Jesus said, "If a man claims to have faith but has no deeds, then what use is it? Faith by itself, if not accompanied by action, is of no worth." Buddha said, "We should never abandon the people of this world, for it is only through service to others that we attain spiritual fulfillment."

November 4ᵗʰ

Humility is the acceptance of the possibility that someone else can teach you something you don't already know, especially about yourself. Conversely, pride and arrogance closes the door of the mind. Lao Tzu said, "To know that you do not know is the best. To pretend to know when you do not know is a disease."

November 5th

We need a healthy body to house the spirit that lives within us. Things such as exercise, eating food that's good for you, yoga, meditation, and massage are all worthwhile. Stress, worry, anger, over-indulging in alcohol or drugs, eating too much, and being overweight are all detrimental to your body. Many people find it worthwhile to fast for a few days, giving the body a light and "high" feeling. One of the most underestimated things is proper breathing, deeply into the stomach and not just the chest. Several times during your day, become aware of your breathing and make sure that you inhale deeply and exhale all of the air from your lungs. Your body also reacts to what's going on in your mind. Think positive thoughts, remove stress, and make every attempt to love and respect all people with whom you come in contact. These are elements in the pathway to good health.

November 6*th*

In a topsy-turvy world, with so much information bombarding you constantly, it's even more important than ever to have faith and confidence in Divine Love. If you can develop this faith, then you'll have nothing to fear. There may be times when you don't know which way to go or which way to turn. When this happens, just stay where you are. Be still and quiet and meditate on the Divine Love, and you'll find how remarkably conditions will work out for you. So much of your life gets in a tangle by your eagerness to get on with something in a big hurry. You only get into a muddle and then have to retrace your steps. Just be still, and trust in the Creator to point the way.

November 7th

If you haven't begun your journey along the spiritual path, now is the time to start. Once you decide to live a more spiritual life, you'll find that every step you take toward the Creator, the Creator will take many more steps toward you. The Great Spirit will not fail to raise you up if you'll just allow yourself to be raised. Any time you turn away from the spiritual life, you'll find yourself back in bondage, in chains. You must eventually throw off all those chains of darkness and see yourself for what you really are. As Carlos Casteneda wrote in *The Teachings of Don Juan,* "Look at every path closely and deliberately before you start to walk it. Does this path have a heart? If you take a path without a heart, it will destroy you. Once you have chosen the right path, jump in, and traverse its full length looking, looking, breathlessly."

November 8th

Don't ever let fear overtake you, for fear can destroy you. You may worry about losing your job, lack of finances, ill health, your children, and many other things. There's always something to worry about, if that's what you're looking for. But you must change your focus from fear to one of thankfulness, being thankful for what you have, and not worrying about what you don't have. Concentrate your heart and life upon the spiritual aspect of your life instead of your material possessions. Remember that your spiritual guides know what your needs are. And what you need will be supplied–not necessarily what you want, but what you need.

November 9ᵗʰ

You may not realize it, but the needs of the planet are the same as the needs of a person. The planet should have the same laws and rights to protection that you have. You want good health and to be free of disease. Well, so does the planet. You don't want your house polluted with unclean air and hazardous waste. Neither does the planet. A proper reverence for the sanctity of the Earth and the diversity of its people is the secret of peace and survival in this world. Your children, your grandchildren, and all unborn generations have the right to an intact heritage, free of contamination. They should be able to enjoy both plant and animal wildlife in the same variety and environment that has existed in the past. It's important that you do your part to see that this happens.

November 10*th*

Often you're caught in a battle of misperceptions. You're told one thing, but then you experience another. People sometimes play with your mind, and some even do it deliberately. You long to believe what you hear. But it's so important to learn to trust your gut feelings. Many times your internal feelings will let you know if someone is not telling you the truth. This is especially true when you're walking down the spiritual path. Why would the Creator have given you your intuition if you're not supposed to listen to it? Don't always believe everything you hear.

"Hearing is not the same as seeing." Swahili Proverb

November 11ᵗʰ

Dogen, a Japanese Zen Master, instructed his monks in the proper way to cook and to do any other kind of work: "Keep your eyes open and do not allow even one grain of rice to be lost. Wash the rice thoroughly, put it in the pot, light the fire, and cook it. See the pot as the inside of your own head. See the water in the pot as your own lifeblood. It is vital to clarify and harmonize your life with your work. Don't lose sight of either the theoretical part of your work or the practical side. Handle even a single leaf of a green in such a way that it manifests the body of the Buddha. This, in turn, allows the Buddha to manifest himself through the leaf."

November 12*th*

There's a Tibetan story that says that being given the opportunity to have a life is about the same odds as a blind turtle surfacing in the ocean inside of a small ring. Life is so rare that it must be cherished and highly prized, and a precious human body is the perfect vehicle for obtaining enlightenment. Some spiritual leaders in the West, on the other hand, regard the body as an obstacle that must be overcome as an impediment. Yet the body holds the potential of being one of your greatest teachers. More than just a mass of flesh and bone, the seven chakras are focal points of energy along the spine. To learn from your body, you should enter into a practice of one of the many mind/body disciplines.

November 13th

Ask any adult in our society if they approve of the way they look. It's rare to find a person who does. The advertising world demands beautiful bodies, and people seem to spend an incredible amount of money trying to make themselves look beautiful on the outside. Think of how beautiful you'd actually be if you spent the same amount of time and money working on increasing your internal beauty. If you'd just work on the spiritual part of yourself, beauty would exude from you. Truly beautiful people attract others because of the beauty within, yet they don't necessarily have external beauty. Remember you're not your body. You are a spirit that will live forever. Doesn't it make more sense to spend more time dwelling on that part of you that is eternal and not the part that is temporary?

November 14th

A teacher honored each of her high school seniors by giving each one a blue ribbon that read, "Who I am makes a difference." The teacher then gave each student three blue ribbons and said to give them to someone who'd made a difference in their lives. One boy gave a ribbon to a company executive for helping him with career planning and told him to give the other two ribbons to anyone he chose. The executive gave one to his grouchy boss and told him to take the other ribbon and give it to someone. The boss went home and gave it to his fourteen-year-old son and said, "I want you to know how much you deserve this." The boy began to sob. He'd just finished writing a suicide note, because he thought his parents didn't care about him. You never know what effect you can have on someone's life by telling a person how much you appreciate him or her.

November 15th

"It's all about me, isn't it?" So many people seem to be preoccupied with themselves. Yet this self-centeredness could prove to be a feature of the search for fulfillment. To find one's self, one must first lose one's self. This is an essential truth that any seeker of self-fulfillment needs to grasp. The Christians say, "The kingdom of heaven is within you." The Buddhists say, "You are the Buddha." Discovering who you really are is the goal of all spiritual journeys. The Japanese Zen master, Dogen, said, "In Buddhism we study the self. To study the self is to forget the self. To forget the self is to be enlightened by all things."

November 16th

A Tibetan proverb says that a Guru is like a fire—you get too close, you get burned, but if you stay too far away, you don't get enough heat. The question is whether or not we need a teacher or a preacher or a Guru to lead us into a spiritual life. The answer to that question is within each individual—obviously some do and some don't. But the most important thing is that your life is moving in a spiritual direction. There are many other sources in order to establish a spiritual path like reading inspirational books by great teachers, listening to others who seem to be on a spiritual path, meditation, prayer, practicing a spiritual life, and doing good works for others.

A story goes that before people populated the planet, Jesus and Satan were talking to each other one day. Satan asked Jesus, "What's life all about?" And Jesus responded, "It's all about love." Satan thought for a minute then said, "Um, that's really good. It sounds like something I'd like to get involved in by organizing it and dividing into different religions."

November 17th

Ecological awareness is spiritual. It's a return to the simple way of life. It's the act of showing a profound respect and responsibility to the earth that our ancestors knew and practiced. Ecological philosophy, like spiritual philosophy, teaches that all things are united in the eyes of God. No matter how deeply one looks into the fabric of material being, it's obvious that life forms are interdependent and co-evolving with each other. Every human effort, thought, and spiritual insight is supported by the whole of organic life. Buddha, Mohammed, and Jesus all went directly into nature to seek answers. The earth teaches us its eternal message, quietly and subtly, unlike learning from a lecture or a textbook. Sun Bear of the Chippewa Tribe said, "I don't think that the measure of a civilization is how tall its buildings of concrete are, but rather how well its people have learned to relate to their environment, as well as to other people."

November 18th

One evening an old Cherokee told his grandson about a battle that goes on inside all people. He said, "My son, the battle is between two wolves inside us all. One is evil. It's filled with anger, envy, jealousy, sorrow, regret, greed, arrogance, self-pity, guilt, resentment, inferiority, lies, false pride, superiority, and ego. The other is good. It's filled with joy, peace, love, hope, serenity, humility, kindness, benevolence, empathy, generosity, truth, compassion and faith." The grandson thought about it for a minute and then asked his grandfather, "Which wolf wins?" The old Cherokee simply replied, "The one you feed."

November 19th

If you see a person in need of help, jump at the chance to do what you can. Doing good deeds for others is important in your spiritual practice. While helping friends is fine, it's even more important to help those who aren't your friends–even strangers and people you don't like. Once you get beyond your own ego and stop thinking about "I" and "Me" and that the world revolves around you, you begin to realize the power of the Spirit working through you. You begin to understand that there is no separation between you and other people except for a different body. The same spirit that inhabits you also inhabits them. And you come to the realization that doing good deeds for others is an act of receiving as much as it is giving.

November 20th

Recently I saw a sign that read "To be a better citizen, do something good for someone who can do nothing for you." Somewhat like, be kind and helpful to others and expect nothing in return, I thought. Jesus took it to an even higher level in his Sermon on the Mount when he said, "If you love those who love you, what reward do you have? And if you salute your brothers only, what have you done that's any different from anyone else?" After reading that sign, I made an effort to be extra kind to those with whom I came in contact, whether I knew them or not, just to try it out. I found that being kind felt so good, I didn't know if I was giving or receiving. Try it and see what happens.

November 21ˢᵗ

Everything you do to or for another person, you're doing it to or for yourself. So remember the Golden Rule and treat others as you would want to be treated. Your separation from others is based on your ego. Your ego needs to always be right, which means if others disagree, they're wrong. Your ego needs to be better, which means if others are not better, then they're not as good as you. Ego needs to be either your way or the highway, which basically means if others choose another way, they're wrong. In order to progress on the spiritual path, you need to work on ridding yourself of your ego and begin treating others as equals–not better than you or worse than you, but the same as you. Be tolerant toward others to let them decide for themselves what is best for them, and then you must be able to accept it.

November 22nd

When you get out of a shower and look into a mirror, what do you see? You see your body in the mirror, but you must always keep in mind that the body you see is not the real you. If you think that what you see in the mirror is you, it will always lead to suffering sooner or later. No matter how good-looking you are now or how physically fit you are now, someday these things will fade and disappear. Your physical body shares the destiny of all forms of life—impermanence and ultimately decay. You must keep in mind that the real you is the spirit that lives within you. If you feed and water and fertilize it, it will always be beautiful. It will never fade away or disappear because that spirit lives forever. You'll one day discard the body, but the spirit is the part of you that you'll carry into eternity.

November 23rd

A group of allied soldiers entered a Buddhist monastery in Burma during World War II because the monks were suspected of hiding some of the fighters who were defending their country. The Lama calmly walked out to meet them. A young soldier ran up to him and was amazed that the Lama put up no defense. "I'm going to kill you," the young soldier shouted. The Lama began to laugh. The soldier shoved the barrel of his rifle against the Lama's forehead. "You can't kill me," the Lama said calmly. The soldier laughed. "All I have to do is pull this trigger, and you'll be dead," he said. The Lama replied, "Oh, you can kill my body. You could even chop it into a thousand pieces with your sword, but you can't kill me. I am not my body. I am a spirit, and my spirit will live forever." The soldier took his rifle down and walked away.

November 24th

Does it feel as if life is racing by at a fast pace? Does it seem that each time you look in the mirror you see an older face? Is there any way to slow time? A lot of the problem has to do with what's happening inside your mind. Time is not going by any faster than it ever did. But sometimes it just seems that way because of busy lifestyles. It helps to find a quiet spot to be alone to think your thoughts. Meditation helps to slow the mind. Attempting to keep your mind in the present is also very important. Try to remember to live in the present as much as possible and never judge what is going on as being good or bad.

November 25th

Every day you will usually have some negative experiences. How you handle those situations says a lot about who you are. It's easy to deal with the pleasant things of life; however, negative things can be used as a challenge and as a teacher. The first thing to do when something negative happens is to say to yourself, "Don't sweat the small stuff." The last thing to do is to get angry. Pass through it, and if you really want to beat the challenge, laugh. If it's a more serious situation, turn to a Higher Power. Reconnect with the Spirit Presence within you and let go of anxious or negative thoughts. Let this Presence raise your understanding and help you put this situation in proper perspective. Learn to be a person who can remain calm and thoughtful about negative things. Realize that these things are teaching you to be a stronger and more resolute person. To become angry is to fail the test.

November 26th

If you could maintain the proper attitude toward life, you could live in harmony with everything. Try today to appreciate the harmony that is available to you only for the taking. Hear it in music, in the colors of the sky, in the trees, in the people you meet. Appreciate yourself as being a valuable element in the harmony of life. Your uniqueness is an essential element in the whole human family and so is the individuality of others. By respecting other people's differences, you enhance the harmony of the whole world. Live in partnership with all of God's creation.

November 27th

When you think of the probability of receiving the life you've been given, it would be more likely that you would win the lottery. In the race of the sperm to the egg, why did yours win? The logical explanation is that you've been given an opportunity to find spiritual enlightenment during this life. Where are you along the path of finding it? You don't have time to waste. Some begin their spiritual journey when they feel something is lacking in their life. One may turn in all directions searching but seeing nothing. Yet intuitively you know that the path you seek is not a strange place but a path home.

November 28th

One way to encourage an attitude of abundance is to be grateful for all that you have rather than focusing on what you don't have. Zen masters see the practice of gratefulness as the essence of their spiritual practice. Being grateful trains you to see all of life as an opportunity. It's easy to feel blessed when you receive, but try the practice of feeling grateful when you give to others without any conditions or strings attached. Money, which has been the slave of man's selfishness, must become the instrument of man's goodwill. Giving to others with no expectation of reward is the essence of unselfish purposes.

November 29th

Sasaki-Roshi, a Zen master, was asked why he had come to travel in America. He responded, "I have come to teach people to laugh." He advises all of his students to start each day by standing straight up and laughing out loud from deep inside the belly. This practice, he says, is equal to an hour of meditation. "Laughter is tremendously healthy. Playfulness is as sacred as any prayer because playfulness, laughter, singing, and dancing will relax you. And the truth is only possible in a relaxed state of being. Since Divine Order is one of acceptance of everything that happens, you may as well burst out in laughter."

November 30ᵗʰ

If you'd let go of the attachment you have to
your possessions and, likewise, let go the attachment you have to your ego then you will have dis-
carded the principle sources of stress in your life.
Renunciation means giving up one's attachment
to the material things of this world an attachment based on the wish to possess them. A Zen
Master remarked, "Renunciation is not giving up
the things of this world, it is accepting the fact
that you can lose them without causing you any
worry. The result of such acceptance brings about
fulfillment, not deprivation." Matthew 6: 19-21
states: "Lay not up for yourselves treasures upon
earth, where moth and rust doth corrupt, and
where thieves break through and steal. But lay up
for yourselves treasures in heaven, where neither
moths nor rust doth corrupt, and where thieves do
not break through and steal. For where your treasure is, there will your heart be also."

December 1st

Do you ever catch yourself telling others what they should do or not do? Words are very powerful, but not nearly as powerful as your deeds. Other people, especially children, pay more attention to what you do rather than what you say. And, furthermore, others are watching you whether you know it or not. So begin your practice today being a good influence on others without using words.

December 2nd

Don't get down and depressed over life. Have confidence and faith in Divine Love. If you don't know what to do, be still and quiet. You'll find how remarkably conditions will work out for you if you stop fretting about them. So much tangle and confusion is made by your eagerness and impatience to move forward. Instead, be still and trust in your Creator.

Paraphrased from the writings of White Eagle

December 3rd

If your goal is to search for the Truth and the Light, you should project thoughts of goodwill and love toward all persons. Always try to see the good in people rather than the bad. Broadcast your love and goodness toward them. Your rays of Light and goodwill toward others will change them for the better. You have no idea how much good you can do by just allowing your higher mind and positive thoughts to dominate your life.

Paraphrased from the writings of White Eagle

December 4th

If you're told to go inside and find your inner space, you may start seeking it like it's an object to be found. If you do this, you'll probably not find it. It's not a detectable object but a spiritual place that dwells within. To find it requires that you shut down your mind, emptying it of all thoughts. You might start by cutting off all outside stimuli and start enjoying simple things like listening to the sound of rain or wind or seeing the beauty of clouds. This begins to open up a space in your mind and closes out the stream of thinking that normally occurs. You will become conscious of being conscious. Say or think "I am" and add nothing to it. Then you'll be aware of the stillness that follows. When you arrive at that place, you'll feel a sense of well-being, as well as a sense of peace.

Paraphrased from the writings of Eckhart Tolle

December 5th

From one point of view, there is neither purpose nor meaning to spiritual discipline for life is sufficient in itself. Another point of view is that "attention" produces "awareness" and thereby awakens the state of mind. By plunging into another dimension of existence through meditation, one usually finds a more intimate place than the "real world." When we commune with it, work is actually done upon our finite personality. We can experience union with something larger than ourselves and in that union find our greatest peace.

Paraphrased from the writings of William James

December 6th

If you are to ever progress spiritually, it is essential that you have respect for all forms of life. You cannot bear ill will toward another or toward any living thing. This creates a polarization in your life that is neither healthy nor good. As Jesus said, you should love your neighbor as yourself, which essentially means to love all people whether you like them or not. To befriend a person you dislike or the one who dislikes you is the foundation of all religions.

White Eagle

December 7*th*

When the concept of peace of mind is introduced and made central to the act of technical work, a fusion of classic and romantic quality can take place at a basic level within a practical working context. You can actually see this fusion in skilled mechanics and the work they do. To say they're not artists is to misunderstand the nature of art. They have patience, care, and attentiveness to what they're doing. But more than that, there's a kind of inner peace of mind that isn't contrived. It results from a kind of harmony with the work in which there's no leader and no follower. The material they are working with, along with their thoughts, interchange in a smooth progression until the mind comes to rest at the exact instant the material is right.

Paraphrased from the writings of Robert M. Pirsig

December 8th

The more you know yourself, the more you come to realize the presence of God within you. Afterwards you begin to realize the presence of God in everyone else. You then begin to feel a bond with others, because of what you have in common with them. The deeper you go inside yourself to commune with the Spirit, the brighter your light becomes. You begin to realize that by opening up, you can allow the light to flow through you and out to others. You will become a light in the land of darkness. And a peace will come over you like nothing you have ever known.

Paraphrased from the writings of K. J. Stewart

December 9th

A *Course in Miracles* tells us that all diseases come from an unwillingness to forgive. In other words, if we are ill, we need to look around and see whom we need to forgive. The one that you find to be the hardest person to forgive is the one you need to forgive the most. Forgiveness means giving up and letting go. It has nothing to do with condoning the action that was inflicted upon you. Once you become willing to forgive, then the Great Spirit will take care of the rest. It's equally important to forgive yourself and to love and respect yourself. When you do this, everything in life seems to work. Love and respect for yourself will improve your health, your relationships with others, and your attitude toward the happenings in your life. Don't criticize yourself. Send positive vibrations to yourself. Understanding and being gentle with yourself is the only way to ever improve.

Paraphrased from the writings of Louise L. Hay

December 10th

Our relationship to the Creator is the same as our relationship with other people. There is nothing we can do for the Creator, but there is much we can do for the Creator's children. As we go about our everyday work, remember to lend a helping hand wherever you can, and know that in so doing, you are fulfilling the will of the Creator. Try to always see the good in others instead of the bad. Every soul on this earth is here by the Creator's Will, and how you act and react toward every soul is your test.

Paraphrased from the writings of Edgar Cayce

December 11th

Most people when they pray have a wish list of things like: "Dear God, please give me good health, please give me happiness, please give me what I want." A much more appropriate prayer would be, "Not my will, but Thou Will be done. I surrender myself to you, dear God, do with me as you will. Help me to do my best, and give me the strength to accept what I am given."

Paraphrased from the writings of White Eagle

December 12th

No matter how much knowledge you may have, the more you progress, the more the horizon recedes. Compared with everything that is possible to learn, human knowledge always remains puny. However, knowing this should not keep you from the pursuit of your spiritual path. You only have so much time, so don't waste it by putting it off. Everything that happens to you is a lesson, sometimes delightful and sometimes painful. This is your life, and you must learn about yourself from yourself. Out of that learning, wisdom comes.

December 13th

All of your life has been based on having a mind that works properly. But you find that as you grow older, you become more forgetful about things that you used to remember. The brain is a muscle and needs to be exercised just like all the rest of the muscles in your body to prevent it from getting weaker. When people begin to have a weakened brain, they sometime develop destructive behavior. By having constructive mental patterns, you will be motivated toward a behavior that will better yourself. Your mind has the capacity to generate new mental impulses and new biological information. When you can retain this creative potential, it is the mark of non-aging. Clinging to old habits, rigid beliefs, and outworn behavior is a sure sign of aging.

Paraphrased from the writings of Deepak Chopra

December 14th

Your mind and your body are in constant communication with each other, even though most of it is on an unconscious level. Are you aware that what you say about your feelings to others may not necessarily be true? But what is more important is what your mind is saying to your body. Try to concentrate each day on sending messages of wellness to your body. Like a cheerleader, urge your immune system to protect you against illnesses and diseases. Send good vibrations to your organs and tell them to keep on working properly. When something actually hurts, avoid becoming absorbed in the pain. Send good messages of wellness to the area of discomfort. Continue daily sending only positive messages, praising your body and thanking it for working well.

Paraphrased from the writings of Bernie S. Siegel, M.D.

December 15th

You pray earnestly for all your problems to be removed. You long for the light and for wonderful spiritual ecstasy. But can you not see that it is by going through the discipline of these outer things that your eyes are opened and your sensitivity to heavenly truth increased? You cannot taste and see until you have passed through this process of discipline. Therefore, thank God for the trials and heartaches, which discipline your soul until it becomes able to comprehend and absorb the beauty of the heavenly life.

Paraphrased from the writings of White Eagle

December 16th

If you want to be on a spiritual path, you must have faith. You must believe very strongly that the way you have chosen is right for you. Prayer is essential, but with prayer, you do all the talking. You must also meditate in order to go inside and listen. Remember that prayer, meditation, regular attendance at church, synagogue, mosque, or whatever is for naught if you don't do service for others. That is the cornerstone of any spiritual path. You must be tolerant and kind toward other people, tolerant of their religion and their pathway. You must not judge other people—they are on their path, and you are on your path. Help those who are less fortunate than you. "Blessed are the poor in spirit, for theirs is the kingdom of heaven." Matthew 5:3

December 17*th*

People always seem to want to be secure. And they seem to have the idea that security comes from having things "nailed down." It's important to learn that security comes from knowing that one always has a place in the movement and the changing of things. Life is in a constant state of flux. When you can no longer hide behind the roles that you play with others, you're forced into presenting your real self to them, which runs the risk of intimacy. Intimacy, real intimacy, is never secure, but is always out of control.

Paraphrased from the writings of Witi Ihimaera, Maori Writer

December 18*th*

Have you ever considered thanking all the people who have treated you badly? Remember that your adversaries are your greatest teachers. You have learned a great deal more from them about yourself than you will ever learn from your friends. Thank them for how crucial they've been in your education. Along the same line, the people who slow us down the most are the ones who are preventing things from happening too quickly. If you were five months pregnant, you would probably want to go ahead and have the baby NOW. But you suffer through the remaining four months and are rewarded at the end with the birth of a baby. Things don't happen when we want them to happen. They happen when they're supposed to happen.

Paraphrased from the writings of Rob Brezsny

December 19th

Be aware that you reap what you sow. Likewise, your mindset can attract what comes into your experience. When you set your TV to channel 12, you normally get the programming that channel 12 provides. If your favorite team is playing football on 105 FM, then when you dial that station, you'll hear the game. This process of attraction can be a powerful influence in your life. Our parents used to tell us that we should always keep our minds out of the gutter and think good thoughts. So if you're attracted to something that is not in your best interest, then you should learn to change the channel. It's best for you to think good thoughts and try to bring into your life what is good for you in the long run and not what is good to you in the short run.

Paraphrased from the writings of Esther and Jerry Hicks

December 20th

It's important sometimes to do a thorough and complete examination of yourself to see if you're on the right path. While there are customs and norms that make sense for you to follow out of consideration for others, you must make sure they're also in your best interests. You must make sure that your identity does not get trapped by them. In examining yourself, you must control and tame your ego and redirect it away from bodily demands, addictions, attachments, and greed. Short-range and immediate desires and gratifications are not, in the long run, in your best interest. You need to maintain some discipline over yourself so that you don't over-eat, don't drink too much alcohol, don't do drugs, don't become lazy or lackadaisical, and don't become overly concerned with your body's wants and desires.

Paraphrased from the writings of Thich Nhat Hanh

December 21ˢᵗ

You are human, but you are also divine. Your purpose for being here on earth is to become less human and more divine. One of the things you must do to accomplish this is to withhold judgment and criticism of others. The human way is to judge in haste the actions of others. The divine way is to remain quiet and loving.

Paraphrased from the writings of White Eagle

December 22nd

As you go about your day's activities, remember to be who you are. Remember that God made you as an individual, different from everyone else, and this was done for a Divine purpose. So, don't try to be or act like someone else. Just be yourself. Let your particular flower bloom to its fullest, with all its individuality. If you are a daisy, don't envy the rose or the gardenia—just be the best daisy you can possibly be.

December 23rd

It's so important to exercise control over your wants and desires. While it's fine to obtain certain things you need to make you happy, continually wanting something new and being dissatisfied with what you already have is the highway to unhappiness. By changing your pattern of wants and desires for things for yourself, try doing service for others. This is what will bring you contentment and happiness. Instead of focusing on what you can receive, try, instead, to look for ways to give to others. There's no reward or even pleasure in storing up possessions of material things. By observing a mastery over your mind and your passions, this will open you up and allow you to begin, perhaps for the first time, to know who you really are.

Paraphrased from the writings of Mahatma Gandhi

December 24th

No matter what may be going on in your life, whether they are good times or bad, chances are it will not last forever. Everything in life is transient. That includes all people, animals, plants, and even mountains and streams. An impermanence prevails in all phases of life. Knowing that, there's no reason to take yourself too seriously. Lighten up and enjoy life without placing yourself in the center of it. No amount of resistance will change this law. So don't become attached to your worldly possessions–they're all transient. This doesn't mean you shouldn't actually enjoy the good that the world has to offer. By not having an attachment to tangible things, it will free you up to enjoy your world from a higher vantage point. You'll be able to appreciate and honor the things of this world without placing an importance and significance that they don't have.

Paraphrased from the writings of Eckhart Tolle

December 25th

A lawyer asked Jesus, "What shall I do to inherit eternal life?"

Jesus answered, "You shall love the Lord your God with all your heart, and with all your soul, and with all your strength, and with all your mind, and your neighbor as yourself."

"And who is my neighbor?" the lawyer asked.

Jesus then told the story of a traveler who was robbed, beaten, and left beside the road. A priest passed him but offered no help. A Levite also passed him without offering help. But a Samaritan, as he passed by, had compassion. He bound his wounds and poured oil and wine on them. He placed him on his own donkey, led him to an inn, and paid the innkeeper for his stay.

"Now which of these three do you believe proved to be a good neighbor?"

The lawyer said, "The one who showed him mercy."

Jesus said, "Go and do likewise."

Luke 10: 25-37

December 26th

With the advent of modern science this society has reached a point that is totally unprecedented on earth. New technologies have been developed that are capable of destroying all life on Mother Earth. The ability to manipulate and control the human mind is steadily increasing. The prospect of genetic engineering of all life forms is already here. We are the first species to ever live that must choose the direction of its own evolution. "With the splitting of the atom, everything has changed save our mode of thinking. Thus we hurl ourselves toward unparalleled catastrophe," said Albert Einstein. A spiritual revolution is needed to save the planet.

December 27ᵗʰ

Do you feel at peace with your life? If not, then you need to practice becoming more spiritual. First, you should discipline your thoughts, your emotions, and your actions. Then strive to have a closer relationship with God and with your true nature. Try to live a natural, wholesome, uncomplicated life. Nurture your body in order to produce good health. Strive to get beyond your ego. Practice humility. Use your intellectual powers and intuition to discern the true essence of your being. Meditate daily to bring about physical relaxation, mental and emotional calmness, and a clear state of awareness. You will know that your spiritual growth is authentic when you realize that you have attained peace of mind.

Paraphrased from the writings of Roy Eugene Davis

December 28th

We all are aware of the force of gravity that keeps us clinging to the side of planet earth. It cannot be seen, heard, or touched, and very few people understand how it works. Until it was discovered by Sir Isaac Newton in the seventeenth century, no one knew gravity existed. There's also a similar force that exists that you may not understand because, likewise, you can't see it, hear it, or touch it. And that force is an ocean of Divine Love that permeates the universe in the same way the sea is invisible to a fish. You have the power to connect with this force by surrendering to it and allowing it to take you over. And if you do, it will change your life forever.

Paraphrased from the writings of Rob Brezsny

December 29ᵗʰ

Try this exercise today and do it all day long. At every opportunity, tell yourself that you are a good person. Keep giving yourself this positive affirmation: "I am a good person." Feel that your spiritual guides are right there with you encouraging you along the way. Know that you are not alone. Feel loved. Feel wanted. Feel needed. Realize that you are made in God's image so how can you be other than good. Be a cheerleader for yourself. That encouragement and love that you give to yourself could change your attitude for the whole day. Afterwards, try to make it a habit.

December 30th

Your Spiritual Report Card Grade yourself A - F

1. Did you work more this year on improving yourself?   ____
2. Are you more loving of yourself and others than you were a year ago? ____
3. Are you spending more time helping other people and less on yourself? ____
4. Are you moving away from an ego-based life with you on center stage? ____
5. Are you still taking yourself too seriously? ____
6. Has your sense of humor improved and are you laughing more? ____
7. Has your faith in a Higher Power increased? ____
8. Are you more willing to let go and let God take over your life? ____
9. Do you feel you know better about who you are this year than you did this time last year? ____

10. Are you now more thankful and appreciative and loving and more fun to be around? ____

11. Are you keeping your body that houses your soul in good shape? ____

12. Are you spending more time in prayer and meditation? ____

13. Have you come to realize that money and materialism should not be your goal in life? ____

14. Are you more flexible, forgiving and tolerant of other people? ____

15. Do you have more patience now than you did last year? ____

16. Are you better able now to put your own death in proper perspective?____

December 31st

New Year's Eve is a time to review the past year. Try to remember what you were like at the beginning of the year. And look at yourself now. Have you changed? Have you improved for the better? Are you more spiritual now than you were a year ago? Are you kinder, more gentle, and more tolerant toward others? Time is moving by at a fast pace. Don't let another year go by without improving the person you are now. Do whatever it takes to be more loving, more spiritual, and more helpful to others. Start making your resolutions for the next year now and exert your self-discipline to stick to them.

Excerpts from writings of the following people were used in the teachings contained in this book for the purpose of illustrating a particular idea or philosophy that has been helpful to my family, my friends, and me:

Andrea Axtell, Nez Perce Elder

Bolles, Richard N., *What Color is Your Parachute?* Ten Speed Press, (1972)

Brezsny, Rob, *Pronoia is the Antidote for Paranoia*, Frog Ltd., 2005

Altona Brown, Athabaskan Elder, Alaska

Buddha, (Siddhartha Bautama founded Buddhism in the 5th century B.C. The word, "Buddha" means enlightened one.)

Bush, Mirabai & Ram Dass, *Compassion in Action; Setting Out on the Path of Service*, Bell Tower, 1992

Callahan, Kathy L., *In the Image of God and the Shadow of Demons*, Trafford Publishing, (2004)

Campbell, Dr. Ross, *How to Really Love Your Child*, Signet Book, (1982)

Campbell, Susan, *The Couple's Journey*, Impact Publishers, (1980)

Carson, Rachel, (1907-1964) *Rachel Carson Quotes*, Marine Biologist

Cayce, Edgar, (1877-1945) wrote over 300 books

Chambers, Oswald, *My Utmost for His Highest*, Dodd, Mead & Company (1935)

Chodron, Pema, "How We Get Hooked, How We Get Unhooked," from *Hooked*, Shambhala Publications, Inc. (2005)

Chogyam Trungpa Rinpoche, preeminent teacher of Tibetan Buddhism

Chopra, Deepak, *Ageless Body Timeless Mind*, Harmony Books (1993)

Cohen, Andrew, Founder of the magazine, EnlightenNext

Cousins, Norman, (1915-1990) Editor of *Saturday Review of Literature*

Das, Shankar, *God Alone Is*, Sadhana Ashram, (1989)

Davis, Roy Eugene, *An Easy Guide to Meditation*, CSA Press, Publishers (1995) and The Science of God-Realization, CSA Press, Publishers (2002)

Deloria, Vine, (1933-2005) Native American Author

Deikman, Arthur J., Professor of Psychiatry, University of California at San Francisco

Dixon, Jeane, *The Call to Glory*, William Morrow & Company (1971)

Dychtwald, Ken, Author of 16 books on aging

Dzogchen Ponlop Rinpoche, born in Sikkem, India, Buddhist scholar and meditation master

Einstein, Albert, (1879-1955) German physicist who developed the theory of general relativity

Faith and Lorraine, Australian Aboriginal Elders

Fields, Rick, *Chop Wood Carry Water*, Jeremy P. Tarcher, Inc., St. Martin's Press (1984)

Fox, Emmet, *The Sermon on the Mount*, Harper and Rowe, (1934)

Freedgood, Maureen, Zen Master

Fromm, Erich, (1900-1980) *The Art of Loving,* Harper and Rowe (1956)

Gandhi, Mahatma from *Thus Spoke Gandhi,* quotes of Mahatma Gandhi, Ruchika Printers (2008)

Gass, Robert, Clinical psychologist and inspirational lecturer in seminars all over the world

Loy, David, teacher of Zen Buddhism, co-authored with wife, Linda Goodhew, *The Dharma of Dragons and Daemons*, Wisdom Publications (2004)

Goodstriker, George, Blackfoot Elder

Geronimo, Apache Warrior

Hay, Louise L., *You Can Heal Your Life,* Specialist Publications (1984) N.S.W. Australia

Hays, Edward, Renowned spiritual guide, a priest for over 50 years, and author of 30 books

Hicks, Esther and Jerry, *The Law of Attraction*, Hay House, Inc. (2006)

Hoblitzelle, Harrison and Olivia, He taught at Columbia, Barnard, & Brandeis Universities, a Buddhist Monk, who taught at the Cambridge Meditation Center. She was a writer, therapist, & teacher.

Hoff, Benjamin, *The Te of Piglet*, Penguin Group (1992)

Ihimaera, Witi, Maori writer

Iyengar, B.K.S., founder of Iyengar Yoga, having taught it for over 75 years, and is a writer of spiritual books.

Jacoby, Robert Peter, Clinical psychologist, authored *The Return to Love*

James, William, (1842-1910) psychologist, philosopher, & author

Jesus, believed to have been born of a virgin, performed miracles, founded the church, rose from the dead, and ascended into heaven, from which he will return. Christians worship him as the incarnation of God.

Ka'ano'i , Patrick, Hawaiian Elder

Kahn, Franklin, Navaho Elder who promoted education and native culture

Keyes, Ken, Jr., *The Hundredth Monkey*, Vision Books, (1982)

King, Matthew, Native American

Kinloch, Patricia, Samoan Doctor

Knight, Charlie, Ute Elder, Native American

Krishnamurti, J., Author of *Think on These Things*

Lao-tzu, Author of *Tao Te Ching*

Lendvay, Susan A., Editor-in-Chief of Venture Inward Magazine

Little Star, Member of the Shawnee Tribe, Native American

Locey, Angeline, Hawaiian Healer

Long Chen Pa, a Tibetan Yogi

Lovelock, James E., English Scientist and Environmentalist

Loy, David and his wife, Linda Goodhew, he an American author and teacher of Japanese Zen Buddhism; she a professor of English Literature

Lyons, Oren, Onondaga Tribal Chief

Macy, Joanna, an environmentalist, author, and scholar of Buddhism

Garcia Marquez, Gabriel, Columbian Nobel Prize Winning Author

Matthew, a tax collector and disciple of Jesus

Mohammed, (570 A.D. – 632 A.D.) Founder of Islam and considered by Muslims to be a messenger and prophet of God

Moody, Raymond, M.D., Psychiatrist and Author of *Life After Life*, Harper Collins, (1975)

Moore, Thomas authored *Meditations, On the Monk Who Dwells in Daily Life,* Harper Collins Publishers

Morgan, Marlo, *Author of Mutant Message Downunder*, Harper Collins Publishers, (1995)

Norberg-Hodge, Helena, Founder and director of the International Society for Ecology and Cultures, author of *Ancient Futures: Learning from Ladakh*, Sierra Club Books, (1991, 2009)

Nouwen, Henri, (1932-1996) Dutch-born writer and Catholic Priest

Peale, Norman Vincent, *The Power of Positive Thinking*, Prentice Hall, Inc., by permission of Peale Center for Christian Living

Pirsig, Robert M., Author of *Zen and the Art of Motorcycle Maintenance*, William Morrow & Co. Publishers, (1974)

Ponder, Catherine, Inspirational author of prosperity books

Prather, Hugh, (1938-2010) author of *Notes to Myself*, Real People Press, (1970)

Rangimarie Turuki Pere, New Zealand Maori, author of *Te Wheke – A Celebration of Infinite Wisdom* (1991)

Rasbash, Jane, Author of article, "Immunology of the Soul," from the Jan/Feb 2002 issue of *In Adoration of Nature*

Ray, Sondra, a California author and self-improvement lecturer

Ring, Kenneth, Professor Emeritus of Psychology at the University of Connecticut and a researcher of near-death experiences

Sakyong Mipham Rinpoche, One of Tibet's most respected incarnate Lamas

Sams, Jamie and David Carson, Native American Writers

Schaef, Anne Wilson, *Native Wisdom for White Minds*, Ballantine Books, (1995)

Shenandoah, Audrey, Onondagan Clan Mother of Navajo descent

Shorter, Wayne, Jazz Saxophonist with Art Blakey's Jazz Messengers in the 1950s, Miles Davis's quintet in the 1960s, and Weather Report in the 1970s

Siegel, Bernie S., *Love, Medicine & Miracles*, Harper Perennial, (1986)

Simmer-Brown, Judith, Chair of Religious Studies at Naropa University, articles published in Shambhala Magazine

Smith, Kara & Ornesha DePaoli, *The Jump Series, Even God Decided to Jump*, unfoldintoONE Publishing (2005)

Snyder, Gary, One of the editors of the *Journal for the Protection of all Beings*

Stair, Nadine, of Louisville, Kentucky, famous for her writing of *If I Had My Life to Live over Again*

Standing Bear, a Ponca Native American chief, who successfully argued in U. S. District Court in 1879 in Omaha that Native Americans are "persons within the meaning of the law" and have the right of habeas corpus

Stewart, K.J., *W.G.O.D., The Revelation Station*, Southern Lotus Media (2006)

Sun Bear, (1929-1992) Chippewa Tribe, Native American Writer

Tarthang Tulku, Tibetan teacher in America, founded Dharma Publishing, organized the World Peace Ceremony, authored over 40 books

Tatanka Yotanka, "Chief Sitting Bull" (1831-1890) led his people in the resistance to the U.S. Government invasion of their territory in the Dakotas

Thich Nhat Hanh, *For A Future To Be Possible*, Parallax Press (1993)

Thurman, Robert, authored several books, taught Tibetan Buddhist Studies at Columbia University, founder and president of the Tibet House New York

Tolle, Eckhart, *A New Earth, Awakening to Your Life's Purpose* (2005)

Twitchell, Paul, *Stranger by the River*, Illuminated Way Press (1971)

Tubesing, Donald and Nancy, authors *of Seeking Your Healthy Balance: A Do-It-Yourself Guide to Whole Person Well-Being*

Turner, Vernon Kitabu, Roshi, Soul to Soul, Hampton Roads Publishing Company, Inc. (2006)

White Eagle, *The Quiet Mind*, The White Eagle Publishing Trust (1972)

White Eagle, *Prayer in the New Age*, The White Eagle Publishing Trust (1957)

Winston, Diana, Co-author of *Fully Present: The Science, Art, and Practice of Mindfulness,* Da Capa Press, (2010)

Wood, Douglas, *The Things Trees Know*, Adventure Publications, Inc. (2005)

Yankelovich, Daniel, graduated from Harvard University, postgraduate studies at the Sorbonne in France, taught psychology at New York University, authored a number of books

Zukav, Gary, *The Seat of the Soul*, Simon & Schuster, (1989)

Made in the USA
Charleston, SC
01 May 2015